A MANAGEMENT GUIDE TO ARTIFICIAL INTELLIGENCE

For Marmalade

A Management Guide to Artificial Intelligence

Tracy Maney and Ian Reid

Gower

© Tracy L. Maney and Ian Reid, 1986

All rights reserved. No part of this publication may be reproduced, stored in a retrieval system, or transmitted in any form or by any means, electronic, mechanical, photocopying, recording, or otherwise without the prior permission of Gower Publishing Company Limited.

Published by
Gower Publishing Company Limited,
Gower House,
Croft Road,
Aldershot,
Hants GU11 3HR,
England

British Library Cataloguing in Publication Data
Maney, Tracy L.
   A management guide to artificial intelligence.
   1. Management — Data processing   2. Artificial intelligence
   3. Business — Data processing
   I. Title   II. Reid, Ian
   658'.0563   HD30.2

ISBN 0-566-02636-8

Typeset in Great Britain by Graphic Studios (Southern) Ltd, Godalming, Surrey. Printed in Great Britain at the University Press, Cambridge.

Contents

Preface		vii
Introduction		1
	Part I Putting AI to Work	
1	Why isn't AI used in business?	11
2	A successful application	16
3	Identifying opportunities	31
4	Assessing feasibility	44
5	Preparing a short list	56
6	Development and implementation	65
7	AI and the small business	78
	Part II AI in Action	
	Introduction to Part II	85
8	Sales and order entry	87
9	Stock control and warehousing	95
10	Credit control	102
11	Management information	111
12	Business planning	119
13	Production scheduling	124
14	Preventive maintenance	129

15	Manufacturing	137
16	Quality control	148
17	Investment decisions	154
18	Fraud detection	162
19	The staff function	169
20	Retail banking	175
References		182
Further reading		183
Index		185

Preface

Many managers feel that Artificial Intelligence (AI) and Expert Systems might be important to their businesses if they knew where and how to use them. This book demonstrates that this belief is correct and explains how to identify real opportunities which can be taken at low risk and cost for early implementation. It also explains why most attempts by businesses to exploit Expert Systems have been unfruitful, highlights the problems to avoid and suggests the controls needed.

The second part of the book identifies and very briefly describes over forty possible opportunities for the profitable use of AI techniques in twelve common business activity areas. This part of the book is included to assist managers in assessing the opportunities in their own businesses.

This book is intended for busy managers who need to know how to use AI but who don't necessarily have time to learn the finer points of the jargon or wish to build their Expert Systems themselves. We hope you find it valuable.

We wish to express our thanks to all those who have helped with this book; to Data Logic Ltd for allowing the methods developed by their employees to be published; and to those customers with whom we learned to practise what this book preaches.

The use of the words 'he' and 'his' in preference to 'he/she' and 'his/hers' is not intended to be sexist and is adopted only as a convenience and to improve readability.

T L Maney
J I C Reid

Introduction

This book explains how artificial intelligence (AI) can be used to improve the profitability of a business. It is based on experience and includes examples which show clearly the competitive advantages now obtainable through the use of well-established technology and for quite modest investment. It explains how to identify those activities in a business where AI is likely to be most cost-effective and how to procure that intelligence. It also explains why the advice given in this book is not more generally known.

This is a book for managers of businesses. Businessmen are generally overworked and have little time to spare. It assumes no initial knowledge of AI and assumes, moreover, that the reader has no desire for any more information on the subject than he needs to evaluate and to procure AI for his business. For those who are interested in constructional details there are many good books available on the technology of AI. Some of these are listed in the Further Reading section at the end of this book.

Part I of the book contains explanations and suggestions on how to identify opportunities to use AI profitably and how to procure those intelligent systems.

AI, expert systems and the like are generally considered by the business world to be advanced techniques which will probably become economically important but which are not yet commercially viable. The typical business view is that a little experimentation in the business may just be worthwhile, but all that can be expected is the development of some trivial toy system.

Chapter 1 explains why so many attempts to use AI in business have failed and so brought about the erroneous view that its techniques are not yet usable. It shows how these failures can be avoided and explains the principles on which this book is based.

Chapter 2 describes one highly profitable example in detail from a managerial viewpoint. This account is included to show that intelligent software can be profitable when correctly applied. The example is very important as it indicates the essential difference between academic research on intelligent systems and the commercial application of AI. This difference must be understood before AI can be introduced into a business successfully.

Chapters 3 to 6 each describe one step of a method which has been used successfully to introduce AI into business. Chapter 3 suggests a means of identifying those points in the business where AI may be cost-effective. It is based on the method developed by the Data Logic Expert Systems group which specialises in the application of expert systems to business problems. The result of this work is a 'long list' of opportunities.

Chapter 4 contains general guidance on how to determine whether a particular application is likely to be feasible. This chapter is not definitive for two reasons. First, there are many special cases and exceptions to the general rules which we do not cover. Second, this is a rapidly developing field. Many of those areas which are not feasible at the time of writing may be practical when the chapter is read.

Chapter 5 covers the selection of one or two intelligent applications from the 'long list' for initial implementation. The method described aids to choosing quick and easy-to-build examples which are also profitable and so provide an easy entry to a new technology.

Chapters 6 and 7 are concerned with implementation

Introduction

or procurement. Chapter 6 is particularly relevant to larger businesses with their own data-processing departments. Chapter 7 addresses the specific problems of small businesses, which may only have a personal computer and cannot justify development costs.

Part II of the book examines a number of commercial application areas and indicates where and how AI might profitably be used. The benefits and the costs will, of course, vary between businesses, and only a few of the many possible application areas are examined. These examples will have direct relevance to some businesses where they may serve as partial checklists. More generally, however, they can be used to indicate the type of area to look out for when assessing other applications.

A note about terminology

As in many other fields, there are no universally agreed definitions of the terms in regular use. A general understanding of the most common terms will suffice, but the reader should be aware that experts in the field will disagree (probably in different ways) with the brief explanations given below. As each term is introduced, its usefulness in business is briefly discussed.

There are two sets of terms in general use. One set is based on the externally perceived operation of a system and the other set derives from the methods of construction used within it. This duplication is a common source of confusion, compounded by the fact that certain internal constructions are closely associated with certain externally perceived functions. This leads to external and internal terms being used as though they were identical and encourages the belief that the only permissible or respectable way to achieve some specific functionality is through the use of a specific constructional method.

The external terms which describe perceived functionality are the most useful to a manager and it is these terms which are used in this book. They are all independent of the methods of construction by which the required functionality is achieved and are therefore less used by AI researchers and workers. They are introduced and explained below.

'Artificial intelligence', or *'AI'*, is an all-embracing term used to label any system that behaves as though it had intelligence. There are many definitions of intelligence, none of which is particularly satisfying. In all cases a system is limited to a particular class of activities, so naturally its 'intelligence' is judged in relation to its performance in that work. There is no universally accepted standard of comparison and no way in which systems can be clearly separated into 'intelligent' and 'non-intelligent'. Under these circumstances the reader is as qualified as any of the experts to consider the results produced by a system and to decide whether or not, in his opinion, that system is 'intelligent' or 'mechanical'.

AI covers a very wide field and includes three areas which are of current importance in business:

- expert systems
- robotics
- language understanding.

'Expert systems' refers to systems which are perceived as acting both intelligently and as though they had expertise in some area of knowledge. Most AI workers believe that to qualify for this title they should be able to explain how they reached their conclusions by producing a reasoned argument incorporating both the data and the knowledge they utilised to reach that conclusion. In this book we relax this definition of 'expert systems' to include those systems which are perceived as reaching intelligent results using expert knowledge but which have no facilities to explain how their conclusions were reached. We have used 'expert systems with explanation facilities'

Introduction

when adhering to the stricter definition of 'expert systems'.

There are several subsidiary classes of expert system. These include:

- The *consultant,* which is intended to have an exceptional level of expertise and to act as an advisor to a human who does not have that high level of expertise. This is the field in which most academic research is now concentrated and represents the generally accepted view of what an expert system should be.
- The *expert interface,* or *intelligent front end,* which is a special sort of consultant. It is expert in the use of some complex computer system or operation and assists an inexperienced user to achieve what he wants. Advanced software designers are now starting to build these expert interfaces into complex systems.
- The *assistant,* which has a lower level of expertise than its human partner, undertakes routine jobs and leaves the human to make the final difficult decisions. This is the easiest and cheapest class of expert system to build and is of particular importance in business. This book is mainly concerned with this class of expert systems.
- The *idiot savant,* which has a small amount of intelligence, a little expertise and a great deal of information. Its task is to use its limited intelligence and expertise to decide what information it should retrieve and offer to its human partner. One typical example of this class of expert system is the maintenance expert which retrieves detailed information on parts of a machine as they are needed.

However, this distinction between expertise and information is not always made, since the whole of the stored permanent data may be regarded as 'knowledge'. It is useful in business to consider them as separate, with 'information' being identical to the data used by conventional systems. 'Expertise' is the different, new part of knowledge which requires special handling.

'Robotics' is the term applied to the study of the control of movement. A robotic system may include a subsidiary expert system if expert knowledge is needed to control the movement. The field is developing fast, but as machines are expensive to design and build, the average business is restricted to buying standard offerings from robot-machine manufacturers. There is, however, sometimes scope for including intelligence in, or for adding to the intelligence of, numerically controlled equipment.

Most tool manufacturers are well aware of the importance of robotics to their future profitability and do not need general advice on this point. No detailed discussion of robotics has been included in this book. However, for those readers who find this field of interest some suggested applications have been included.

Speech recognition is not fully developed, although it is advancing quickly. There are several circumstances in business where the little that can be done can be used effectively and to considerable advantage. As this book is concerned with what can be done at the time of writing and not with future possibilities, it is likely to understate the potential of such a fast-moving area. A convenient rule of thumb by which to judge progress is that if there is a speech-driven word processor on the market at the time of reading, then much more can be accomplished within this field than is stated in this book.

The internal terms, derived from the constructional methods used, are not as important to the purpose of this book as the perceptual or functional terms. However, it may be useful to have a brief explanation of the most commonly used words.

Conventional programs include conditional tests

Introduction

which are used to determine the action of the program. For example, a payroll program might be required to pay an additional £1 each week to employees who hold first-aid certificates and would then include within it some statement such as, 'If employee is first-aider, then add 1.00 to gross pay'. Intelligent systems include large numbers of *rules* which govern their operation. Those rules are, broadly speaking, similar to the condition/action statement described above.

When the rules are separated from the rest of the program, the collection of rules is known as the *'rule base'*. Most expert systems store their expert knowledge in the form of rules in a rule base, which is then often known as a *'knowledge base'*. From this is derived the term *'intelligent knowledge-based system'*, or *'IKBS'*, which is often used as synonymous with 'expert system'.

When the rules are separated from the program, the remainder of the system which uses the rules if often called an *'inference engine'*. This term is sometimes used for the software alone, sometimes for the combined computer hardware and software. A program which operates on a rule base but which is supplied without any rules, analogous to a conventional software package which its user tunes by giving values to control parameters, is known as a *'shell'*. Shells often come with tool sets to help build up a rule base, to simplify print formating and so on.

Knowledge is not always stored as rules. Sometimes related knowledge is stored in blocks for convenient handling. One class of knowledge block is known as a *'frame'*.

Special computer languages have been produced to reduce the cost and times required to program an intelligent system. These languages work on lists of information which define categories of, and relationships between, objects.

The AI programmer uses these languages to inform the

system of the relationships between objects (hence the term *'object-oriented language'*), and he spends little if any effort in instructing the system on the sequence of operations which are to be carried out. There are many AI languages, the most famous being *PROLOG* and *LISP*.

Summary

This book explains how AI can be used to improve profitability. It suggests how to locate suitable areas in a business where AI may be beneficial and it includes a number of examples.

The principal terms used in the book are all perceptual, and the following are discussed:

- artificial intelligence – describing the whole field
- expert systems – which comprise knowledge as well as intelligence
- consultant expert systems – stand-alone, hard-to-build, state-of-the-art advisors
- assistant expert systems – undertaking the intelligent donkey work for a human partner
- idiot savants – with just enough intelligence to know what information or calculations their human partner needs and provide a service (midway between assistant and interface)
- expert interfaces – which help non-experts use other systems
- robotics – intelligent movement, which has limited application
- speech recognition – which can be useful even though currently limited.

PART I
PUTTING AI TO WORK

1 Why Isn't AI Used in Business?

This book claims that the profitability of many businesses can be improved at relatively low cost through the use of AI in appropriate places. Yet there are very few reports of businesses using AI, and those which do are apparently only using it for very unusual areas where they make practically no impact on profitability. Most readers will know of businesses which have investigated the use of AI. Some firms have instructed an employee to look into it, while others have employed consultants who are known to be authorities in the field. The result has almost always been the same: a mildly interesting, 'toy' expert system which runs on a special computer and serves no practical purpose.

What is different about the advice given in this book?

This is quite clearly a vital question which deserves a full answer. It would be true to say that there are a small number of businesses which do use AI very effectively to obtain an advantage over their competitors, and quite naturally they do not publicise the fact. If asked, they will suggest that they tried and the experiment was not productive. Examples of the general class of successful commercial intelligent systems are given later. In this chapter we give the reasons why, in our view, most attempts at using AI in a commercial environment fail and also *what we believe* to be the alternative path which leads to success.

The early workers who first tackled the problem of developing intelligent systems were primarily interested in how intelligence could be built into a computer rather than in how that intelligence could be most effectively used for commercial purposes. They had to solve two difficult problems; namely, how to capture and store knowledge and how to make use of that knowledge to solve new problems in an intelligent manner. They were concerned with the development of new methods and techniques, and therefore they reduced any extraneous development to the minimum possible. One area which they so reduced was that by which information on a particular problem is presented to the 'intelligence' and that by which its conclusions were reported. It was much easier for them to use a keyboard and screen whereby they could see and control both the input and the output.

This is the reason why AI was originally developed in 'stand-alone' systems rather than as units within conventional systems. Naturally the work was easier when the information volumes were small, since no one enjoys keying in large volumes of data. Thus AI techniques were initially developed to handle small volumes of data.

The early work demonstrated that software tools such as PROLOG and LISP would ease the building of intelligent systems. The tools were to be used primarily by research workers who wanted stand-alone, low-volume systems. The tools which were produced did not therefore include provisions for incorporation in conventional high-volume systems, and thus the thinking and the development of stand-alone systems was perpetuated.

Computer-hardware manufacturers have seen that almost all intelligent systems are stand-alone. They have assumed that this is what is required and so have developed special hardware with special operating

Why Isn't AI Used in Business?

systems ideal for research workers. This special equipment is very difficult to incorporate into the heart of a conventional commercial business system since it lacks the data-base utilities and other services which conventional systems need.

The task of problem solving may use four separate functional entities:

- the 'intelligence' or deductive capability required
- the necessary expertise
- reference information relevant to the task
- information about the particular problem in hand.

Two additional factors are relevant when a sequence of similar problems is to be solved. These are:

- the speed at which solutions are required
- the total number in the sequence.

The effort required to solve any sequence of problems depends on these six factors in combination. The benefit obtained from a computer system will remain approximately constant if one factor is reduced in difficulty and another is increased to the same extent.

If the input facilities are limited and there is no sophisticated data-base software available to provide reference data storage, then the last four of the six factors listed above are constrained. Thus, to obtain a significant benefit the remaining two factors must be extensive. These two are the reasoning capability and the expertise of the system. This leads to the usual conclusion that expert systems can only be beneficial if they are *'expert consultants'*.

There are three serious disadvantages in concentrating entirely on highly expert consultants in a business environment. First, there are usually few places in a business where a high level of expertise is desirable; most of the work is basically repetitive and uses quite modest amounts of expertise and intelligence. Second, those fields where a very high level of expertise would be beneficial are those fields where expertise is difficult to pin down and where experts who can advise are rare. Third, it may easily require several years of hard work to collect the expertise needed, and often it is beyond current capability to build such a system.

This is, however, the normal approach adopted when considering the introduction of AI into a business. The AI expert and the staff member with whom he works both look for rare skills to encapsulate in an expert system. They implement an initial model using a stand-alone shell or language which will not communicate with the rest of the business systems, and in most cases that is as far as it goes.

The alternative path is now obvious. Don't look for rare skills and experience or for high-intelligence opportunities. Look instead for those places where a reasonable level of expertise is used (or would be valuable) on high-volume work. Then aim for an assistant expert system which only undertakes the most straightforward of the intelligent tasks and which calls on its human partner to hand the difficult work. The benefits of this approach are:

- An improvement in the work undertaken. Systems do not change their application of knowledge after lunch, a hard day or an argument.
- It is possible to apply reasonable intelligence to improve high-volume tasks which are already performed mechanically.
- There are usually many candidate places in any business where such intelligence would be beneficial. One can choose the most cost-effective to start with.
- There is no need to use state-of-the-art technology. Some well-established method, no longer of interest to the AI research workers, will usually suffice.

Why Isn't AI Used in Business?

- The system can be built and be in use in, say, six to nine months rather than in years.
- Such systems are much simpler and so less likely to contain errors.

Once one or two simple AI systems have been built, experience has been gained and viability proved, a business might start on the long and arduous task of building a full expert consultant. There are situations where they can be profitable. However, they are not a good place to start, and they do not offer a quick return.

Why isn't everybody following this approach?

There is no very satisfying answer to this question. There are a few AI groups which have been working on these lines for some time, but they have avoided publicity to preserve their own markets. The authors, who work for such an organisation, have only recently been given permission to publish this book, so presumably it is expected that this method will soon be more widely known and used. The remainder are presumably misled by the fact that AI is generally thought of in terms of the large stand-alone expert consultant of AI research. Once one is given the 'stand-alone' path to explore, one tends not to search for easier but less exciting routes which lead to the same end.

Summary

Most attempts to introduce AI into business fail because they assume that benefit demands high technology and very ambitious objectives. There is a place for these, but there are more places more easily filled using the small, simple, embedded assistant subsystems.

2 A Successful Application

This chapter presents a case history covering the identification and construction of an AI subsystem to meet a business need – that of reconciling banking nostro account details and statements. The case history is presented from the business viewpoint; technical details are given only at the level which was required by the decision makers actually involved and are not sufficient to enable a similar system to be built. A technical paper which explains the construction details of this example has been produced and is listed as item (1) in the reference section on page 182.

This case history is included for two reasons. The first is to demonstrate beyond all reasonable doubt that AI technology can be used *now* to improve profitability provided that one knows where and how to use it. The development work in this example took about three months to complete and, when applied in a medium-sized organisation, can achieve complete payback in the first two months of operation. The second reason is to illustrate the development of a commercial expert system and so provide backing and understanding to the next four chapters.

This example is unusual in that the application was identified more or less by accident rather than as the result of a deliberate search within a business for fields where AI techniques might make a significant contribution to business profitability. In other respects the application is reasonably typical.

A Successful Application

The example begins with a description of the business need for those who may be unfamiliar with the task of banking nostro reconciliation; then follows the history of the case through to implementation.

The business need

When one bank agrees with another to transfer funds, each bank makes a record of that agreement. For example, when two foreign-exchange dealers agree on a deal by telephone, each of the dealers makes a record of his understanding of the deal. In the case of foreign-exchange deals the most important details are the amounts and currencies involved, the date on which payments are due and, of course, who the correspondent was in the deal.

The records produced by the dealers are entered into the bank's accountancy systems and held as entries in a ledger of the bank's accounts with other banks. That ledger is usually known as the 'nostro' ledger. Copies of entries in the nostro ledger are sent as 'statements' to the correspondent banks. Statements may be sent by letter or by telex but the majority are transmitted through a banking network system known as SWIFT or through group networks where they are stored on magnetic tape upon arrival.

There are several opportunities for errors to be made in the course of preparing interbank accounts. Deals may go unrecorded during a spell of rapid dealings, there may be misunderstanding between the dealers, misrecording of a deal, loss of a deal slip, transcription errors and so on, any of which may result in an error in the nostro ledger and the consequent non-payment of a very large sum by the due date. Delayed payment incurs heavy penalties in interest charges, so each bank reconciles the statements it receives with its own nostro ledger accounts to detect any incompatibility between them.

The reconciliation process traditionally comprises three steps. In the first step any statements and nostro entries exactly matching each other are paired up and written into a history file. In the second step both sets of remaining records are printed out in various sequences and reconciliation clerks attempt to find pairs or groups which are clearly intended to match but which do not match exactly. Inexact matches may be of several classes. Each record includes two reference fields, one of which should contain the reference allocated by the bank which owns that account and the other by the bank which services it. A reference may differ because in one case there are slashes between groups of letters whereas in the other there are commas or spaces; a single character may have been omitted, two adjacent characters may have been transcribed or any other spelling or transcription errors may have occurred. Sometimes a field is not completed at all, sometimes the contents of the two reference fields are interchanged. The amounts fields may differ by a small value due to a rounding difference, the inclusion of a handling fee and so on. The dates may differ because the European sequence of DDMMYY or the American sequence of MMDDYY has been used instead of the required YYMMDD. Sometimes the statement may consolidate two or more nostro entries or *vice versa*. The third step is to investigate those records which still remain unmatched after the inexact matching process is complete. It involves telephone and written enquiries and is the step which reveals the true errors which have been made.

The size of the task varies, of course, according to the volume of business done by the bank with other banks. The number which match exactly depends both on the bank and on the correspondents they normally use, but it can be as low as 40 per cent of the total. A large bank may therefore have, say, 6000 new entries added each day to

A Successful Application

the nostro and the statement files for which there is no exact match. Records are seldom cleared by inexact matching on the day on which they arrive. If the average 'stay' is three days, then to keep up with the work flow the reconciliation clerks may need to search through two listings each containing 18 000 records and find 6000 in exactly matching pairs every day. When the attempts to find an inexact match are exhausted, the third step of detailed investigation can begin.

It is not surprising that with these volumes most banks are unable to detect all the errors in time to avoid occasional interest charges. The sums involved are usually in multiples of £1 million and typical interest payments due to these undetected errors over a period of a year are from £200 000 upwards. Most of these interest payments could be avoided were it possible to undertake the inexact matching process more quickly.

The inexact matching has other effects on profitability. Until the items in the nostro ledger have been reconciled, the bank cannot be certain that it has an accurate picture of its position in various currencies. It may be exposed to risks from currency fluctuations of which it is unaware. The ledger may show that deals have been offset for futures, buys against sells, so that the bank is at no risk from currency fluctuations. If one record for, say, £5 million has been misrecorded as a buy when it should be a sell, the bank will actually be exposed to the tune of £10 million. The sooner an undesired exposure is found and corrected, the lower the risk of heavy loss. The third disadvantage of manual inexact matching is small by comparison to the previous two, yet still significant. Manual inexact matching is labour intensive and expensive. Many banks have large reconciliation departments which could be reduced were the matching process more efficient.

Identification of an AI opportunity

This application is a clear candidate for assessment as to the suitability of an AI solution for the following reasons:

- The reconciliation task uses the output from a computer system, (the nostro ledger), a prime location to examine when searching for possible AI opportunities.
- The knowledge used by the reconciliation clerks is extensive but only a small subset of that knowledge is used during inexact matching, an area which can be isolated easily as it is already a separate step of the whole process.
- The through-put requirements are high, often higher than the human clerks can handle within the allowable time.
- The benefits to be gained from any solution to the current problem are large, approaching £1 million per annum for large banks from reduced labour costs, interest charges and risks from unidentified exposures.
- Conventional software techniques have not proved capable of a fully effective solution.
- Finally the 'rules' used in inexact matching are easily found. The reference field inexact match requirements are closely related to the problem of spelling correction which is well researched, and the inexact amount matches lie within the equally well-established field of fuzzy searching. Had a good AI survey team examined the application, they would almost certainly have identified it as suitable.

What actually happened was as follows. A number of banks wanted to replace their existing conventional reconciliation system with software which would run on IBM hardware. They also wanted a system which would accept input 'on line' from the SWIFT interface device

A Successful Application

and produce the listings used for manual matching on request rather than solely on an overnight batch run. They asked Data Logic if they had such a package. Since Data Logic did not, analysis and design studies were commenced with a view to producing a package with the properties desired. The initial design was complicated by the need to provide for systems of various through-put capabilities which might require a system 38 or a 4300 series and possibly other IBM vehicles as well. These computers have different characteristics, and a design which suits one may not suit another. If different designs were to be used for different through-puts, the package prices would be higher. The problem was therefore referred to Data Logic's software engineering department for consideration. This department included staff with AI skills, and it provided a twofold recommendation. The first was to use an atomic software design (ie one composed of small self-contained pieces) which would operate either on networked IBM PCs or on a mainframe, and the second was to investigate the possible use of embedded expert systems to find inexact matches.

Redefining the requirement

Systems which incorporate expertise are often quite different from conventional systems, and the specification produced for a conventional system is not necessarily suitable for an expert system. In this case a principle objective of the conventional system was the production of listings in various sequences to facilitate manual inexact matching. If the system was itself capable of finding inexact matches, there would be less need for such listings, but there would be a new need; namely, some means of presenting proposed matches and the reasons for those matches being suggested to the reconciliation clerk for approval or rejection.

There were other less immediately obvious consequential changes. The clerk would in future spend a larger proportion of his time examining and dealing with a much smaller set of outstanding unresolved cases. He and the system would work much closer together, and he could be given additional conventional technology support in that work, particularly if he operated on the outstanding records through a terminal. Though the details are not relevant to the expert system element, they are of interest in that they illustrate the side effects which can and often do arise when the nature of a supporting system is changed.

Instead of working with long listings to identify matching pairs or groups and then entering in the six-digit identifiers of matched records through a terminal, the clerk works almost entirely directly with the terminal, where records are identified by their position on the display – a single character entry rather than six digits.

Listings can be produced when required, but this method of operation is exceptional. The terminal is actually a PC connected by a network to other reconciliation PCs and to a number of servers. The screen shows on the top line a synopsis of the overall position of that PC; for example, counts and values of records in and out, record priority warnings and the like. The clerk has three main tasks. The first is dealing with high-priority unmatched records. As he takes actions he can impose a delay on the record, which allows him to be informed if the record has still not been matched when the delay expires. The system tracks and records actions, produces pre-formatted letters and memos for post, telex or other transmission, and in general supports his activity. His second task is to attempt to find those matches which the machine has missed, using his more extensive knowledge and greater intelligence.

A Successful Application

He can, if he chooses, take prints of the remaining records and search them as he would previously have done, but he can do it more easily using the terminal. For this task the screen is split into two vertical columns, one for each file. The records are displayed as though they were attached to two fruit-machine wheels which he can rotate separately, up or down, one record at a time or more quickly. He can lock records in position and move the remainder by depressing two keys – he can free them, build several into a possible match group and see the outstanding balance and so on. He uses the keyboard as though he were controlling an arcade game. He need not move his hands; he need only depress the appropriate finger.

His final main task is to inspect the inexact matches found by the machine which have a match probability lower than a preset threshold. He is asked in each case to accept or to reject the match proposed, but he may also defer his decision if he wishes. The resultant requirement specification is very different from that which was previously prepared when only conventional methods were contemplated.

Establishing the rules

In this example there was no doubt that the expert systems required could be built, and it was decided to separate the production of the software into two parallel activities. The greater part of the work was the detailed design and construction of the bulk of the system using conventional methods. This was produced using methods and tools which could have been used for any other normal system and is not discussed further here.

In parallel with that activity, work commenced on the expert subsystem which would be needed to carry out inexact matching. It was decided to use several small ones, each handling a particular task, so that searches for matches could be carried out as a series of searches which could be called for in any desired sequence. A similar design had previously been produced for reconciling invoices and payments for a factoring company which had been having difficulty allocating bulk payments to individual client's invoices. There were differences, however; so the first task was to define a set of rules which would suit the nostro system.

A prototype was built using PROLOG on a PC. This was a stand-alone prototype; the records to be compared were typed in through the keyboard. It was not efficient in its speed of operation, but it provided an easy means of trying out and adjusting the proposed rules of matching.

The approach involved the prototyping of three expert subsystems which each handled part of the task. There is no need here to follow the development of all three, so further discussion is limited to the most interesting, which was the one charged with the inexact matching of reference field contents. This was required to compare two fields and to search for identical character sequences which might be preceded by, include or be followed by one or more errors of the following types:

- additional characters
- omitted characters
- mismatching characters
- character inversions.

Though simple for a human, this is quite difficult to define in a set of rules so as to achieve a human-like interpretation. A single sheet of paper containing a list of rules seems a poor return for some twenty days of intensive effort and careful thought, so it is worthwhile exploring the difficulties a little before going on. One or two examples may help. Consider the two character strings A B C D E and A B D F E. We can arrange one

A Successful Application

over the other to compare the two thus:
```
A B C D   E
A B   D F E
```
Clearly the second string in comparison to the first contains an omission and an additional character. The 'C' is omitted and the 'F' is an addition. Now suppose that the second string were A B F D E instead of A B D F E. We could present this as an addition and as an omission; we have only placed the 'F' before the 'D' instead of after it, giving the first of the two pairs shown below. Yet a human would prefer the second illustration where the 'F' is treated as a mismatch for the 'C'.
```
A B C   D E     A B C D E
A B   F D E     A B F D E
```
The rules which define omission and addition must recognise this simple exception. The first matching method shows two errors; the second only one.

Now return to the first example. This has been presented as an addition and an omission, yet it would also be interpreted as a character pair reversal and a mismatch of 'C' for 'F'. Why is this not appropriate? The answer is that humans would take the simpler explanation. Finally, consider a partially repeated string; for example, A A B C D compared with A B C D. A human would regard the first A as additional rather than the second, giving:
```
  A B C D           A   B C D
A A B C D  rather than  A A B C D
```
whereas a conventional computer system would suggest the second pattern.

The above example illustrates the adjustments which were needed to tune the expert system and so produce a satisfactory result. The tuning process demands careful thought and experiment and so takes time.

Each class of error and the number of errors in the fields could be used to determine the probability that the two records were intended to be a match. For example, single-character omissions and additions are both rather more common errors than a two-character reversal, but two separate mismatches are less common than a two-character reversal. Thus a preliminary match probability can be derived by counting the errors of each type which are found and allocating a probability accordingly.

There is, however, a second level of probability allocation which can be included. When two characters mismatch it may be because a manuscript character was badly drawn and misread or because a keying error occurred. There are pairs of characters which are particularly likely to be misread; for example, 'B' and '8'. There are certain miskeying errors which are more probable than others: 'B' and 'V' are adjacent on the keyboard, and only a very small variation in the hand movement from the 'home' position can cause one to be keyed when the other was intended. 'A' and 'Q' are also neighbours, but 'A' is a 'home' key and it is much less likely that 'Q' will be struck when 'A' was intended than that 'B' will be struck instead of 'V'. A table of possible mismatch pairs can be produced in which the probability of each possible mismatch can be entered. If this is done, the expert system will use knowledge which is known to be rarely used by the human experts and so can make a better choice than the human between alternative pairings.

The work went quickly because there was already a good foundation from earlier tasks. Had it been started from scratch, it would probably have taken two people about three or four weeks to get a working set of rules.

When each prototype was working satisfactorily in a PROLOG implementation, the rules were established, but the prototype software was unusable; an embedded, fast-operating system was needed and the prototype was neither. The rules had to be used to build working versions.

A Successful Application

Designing the operational expert subsystem

The inexact reference field matcher must be sufficiently efficient to handle a very large number of comparisons each day. Each incoming record which does not match exactly may require comparison with several thousand records on the 'opposite' side; that is, each statement may have to be compared with several thousand nostro records and *vice versa*. As the system may receive several thousand records each day which do not match exactly, the total number of comparisons required can be in the millions. This is a very different loading from that normally envisaged for expert systems of the stand-alone type, and special care must be taken with software design.

In this application the expert subsystem is searching for possible matches – records which match within some predetermined probability threshold. There is no need to continue comparison of records which are found to lie outside that threshold, and thus the design should cause the rejection of unsuitable pairings at the earliest possible occasion. The design aim must therefore be to construct a sequence of sieves each of which rejects unacceptable records and only passes on to the next stage those pairings or groupings which justify further work. Each intermediate sieve can be more searching and less efficient than its predecessors. The final sieve will then only handle a very small proportion of the total through-put and so can carry out the most sophisticated processing without disadvantage.

Several alternatives were considered for the first and most critical sieve. This sieve would be used many times for every incoming record and so had to be designed for implementation in a high-efficiency conventional language using the smallest possible number of instructions.

One possibility considered was to prepare a map for each reference field in which the presence or absence of one or more characters from a group was represented by a '1'. Thus if sixteen indicators were allowed for each reference field, each indicator would indicate the presence or absence of any one or more characters from groups of two or three characters. Thus a '1' might be shown in the first position if the reference field contained one or more from the letters 'A' and 'Q' and the digit '7'. These indicators would only be established once for each field at the start of the matching process and could then be used to reject possible matches in which, say, two or more differences were found in the two sets of indicators.

The actual details of the design work which led to the eventual selection of a set of sieves are not relevant here. It is sufficient to appreciate that though the software involved in each is small and the techniques are taken from software engineering rather than from AI, the design work is critical to obtaining a high through-put. This design work also results in some of the rules being incorporated in conventional software. An AI language such as PROLOG cannot be used. Such software is produced more slowly than normal application software; don't expect the number of lines per day that would be appropriate for a COBOL accountancy program.

The final operation, which would only operate on pairs which were known to be reasonably good matches, could have been implemented in PROLOG and still have achieved the required speed. However, it was decided that it would be easier for maintenance programmers if the final group of matching and interpreting rules were also implemented using the same conventional language as the rest of the system. Further details are given in (1) in the references section at the end of this book.

A Successful Application

Testing the design

Once the expert subsystem design was complete, it was implemented in Pascal, a conventional programming language, and a small set of data handling routines was built around it to enable it to be tested. The reference field matcher comprised some 900 lines of source code and the testing framework about 300 lines. These took about three weeks to write. This software was used as a second-stage prototype; the tests were more concerned with ensuring that the results were equivalent to those of a human reconciliation clerk than to ensuring that the functionality of the new version was identical to that of the initial PROLOG prototype. The system was demonstrated to reconciliation clerks, and as a result some minor amendments were made.

Implementation

The completed expert subsystems were disconnected from the test harness software and passed to the conventional software development team for inclusion in the system as subroutines. The remainder of the work was then no different from that of a normal software development.

Development effort

The total effort used to redefine the requirement specification to take advantage of the included AI capability, to establish the rules, build the first prototype, design, build and test the second and hand over the routines was approximately twenty-five intensive man-weeks. In this case there were no changes required to existing systems since the surrounding software was all new.

Assessment of the case history

The annual benefit from the system depends on the size of the operation. For large operations it could be as much as £500 000 savings on interest payments, reduced exposure to risk from currency fluctuations and from reduced costs. The investment in the development of the AI subsystems, assuming fee rates of £500 per day for first-class commercially experienced AI workers, would be about £60 000. The development period is about three months, assuming a team of two workers. The risks of the development are low since the technology and the 'rules' are well established. There is no alternative using conventional methods; if there were, it would have been used years ago.

It should also be stressed that this example is not an unusual application; reconciliation of one form or another is a very common process. There has been no cheating, no use of a special and rare task without general application to strengthen the argument expressed in this book. The example chosen is a fair representation of what can be achieved.

This case history is quite obviously an example of a commercially viable 'expert system' solution to a genuine business problem. The authors claim that it is not possible to look at this example and then to argue that AI technology is not yet sufficiently developed to have any significance to business profitability, or that any worthwhile system takes years to develop. The opportunities are there now if you know how to identify and how to exploit them.

3 Identifying Opportunities

This chapter discusses the ways in which business opportunities for the effective use of artificial intelligence may be identified.

The task is difficult if you don't know what to look for or what AI can and can't do. It demands an understanding of what can be expected from AI technology, an understanding of the needs and operations of the business and the ability to isolate existing tasks which can increase profitability if performed by an intelligent process. It also demands the ability to visualise how the business might be operated if machine intelligence were increased, since often the most significant benefits accrue from using AI to perform work which has not previously been a practical subject for AI application. Those who work in a business are so familiar with its current operations and methods that they find it extremely difficult to see alternatives. Just as only the visitor notices the tick of a clock which the residents do not hear, so it is difficult for those inside a business to notice the possible changes which AI can make to their work.

This suggests the use of an external consultancy, but there are very few consultants who have real experience in the application of AI to business problems. The majority of AI consultants have a knowledge of AI but not of business applications, and they tend to think in terms of large stand-alone systems.

This book will help managers to know what to look for.

The discussion on application areas in Part II will familiarise them with the thought process required, but there remains the question of determining how a business may be surveyed in a systematic manner to produce a list which includes the majority of the cost-effective opportunities. This chapter is based on experience from a number of such surveys and describes the methods found most effective by Data Logic AI survey teams.

Alternative approaches

The alternative approaches which may be used to identify suitable opportunity areas include:

- tasking an employee to learn the capabilities of AI and to identify suitable areas
- employing an in-house AI expert
- tasking the systems development staff to examine some or all applications and to list suitable areas
- identification of suitable areas by departmental managers
- identification by senior management working groups
- survey by external consultants.

External consultants can also be used in conjunction with any of the first five approaches.

Each approach has its advantages and disadvantages which are discussed briefly below. Subsequent sections describe in more detail the approach which has been found to be successful. The authors work for a consultancy company and therefore have no direct experience of surveys carried out completely in-house; naturally the method recommended assumes that consultants will be employed. However, for those who decide to work unassisted there are some tentative suggestions on how this might best be done.

Identifying Opportunities

Tasking an existing employee

This approach is cheap but has not proved very successful. AI covers a wide field, most of the available literature assumes previous knowledge and several months of reading would be needed to familiarise oneself with what has been done. There is not nearly enough information on how to apply research work to real applications. Thus the employee starts looking without any clear idea of what he is looking for.

The second difficulty is that very few employees have a real understanding of the whole business. Even those who know much of what is done in the business may not know how changes to it will alter profitability nor where the major business threats, opportunities and constraints lie. Finally, one person working alone who is familiar with the business will find great difficulty in examining it from a totally new viewpoint.

When a list of possible applications is produced by an employee it is difficult to decide what to do with it. There may be doubts as to whether the opportunities identified are feasible, profitable and so on, since the employee will lack credibility within the organisation as an authority in the AI field. The result has been that even when suitable opportunities are identified, little is done with them.

It is hoped that this book will assist the tasked employee to identify suitable opportunities and also help his management to appreciate them, thus making this approach more effective than it has previously been.

Employing an AI expert

Most AI experts are specialists in particular areas of what is now a very wide field. They are scarce and they are expensive and the rarest of all are those who specialise in using the existing techniques. Moreover, many of them have entered AI work without a business grounding and they lack the almost intuitive appreciation of costs and income that is the other prerequisite of the task.

Although they are specialists, they will, however, have the necessary general knowledge of their field, and they should be able to learn quickly, provided that their need for help in understanding the business is appreciated and met. This approach can be successful when the AI expert works with a partner who knows the business well and has access to other AI specialists as needed.

Using the systems development staff

The benefits gained by using the systems development staff, where they subdivide the work according to those parts of the business which they normally support, accrue because of three main factors. First, each has, or should have, a detailed knowledge of his part of the business, which extends beyond a knowledge of what is now done. He should also know what is needed and the business factors which determine profitability. Second, as each only examines his own part of the business, he is likely to examine that part in more detail. Finally, since there are several people working on similar problems, they can 'walk through' their findings with one another and so produce a better result.

The first disadvantage, as with a single employee, is the problem of learning enough of the capability of AI to identify what may be possible. The disruption to the analyst's normal work may represent an unacceptable cost. The second disadvantage is that since each analyst examines his own area and not the whole business, attention is directed within the boundaries of those areas. This may result in the omission of opportunities

Identifying Opportunities 35

which span boundaries and are thus not seen unless the business is examined as a whole.

Departmental managers

Departmental managers should know the needs and constraints of their business areas and would be ideal people to identify opportunities – if they had the time to learn how AI can be used and to decide how to apply it. One purpose of this book is to convince them that this time might be well spent; a second purpose is to give them the information they need to understand the uses of AI and to produce an AI wish-list for their own operational field.

Even if that purpose is fulfilled, we are still exposed to the possibility of overlooking significant opportunities because, instead of fitting neatly into sections of the business, they span several departments.

Senior management

Senior managers have very little time and should not have to undertake a full survey. They are, however, often the only people who can see the whole business in balance, so their input is particularly vital.

Outside consultants

Outside consultants cannot work without contact with the business's own staff. They will be very pleased to carry out a complete survey, visiting each department, learning what it does and then assessing where AI might be used. This can be useful but is often unnecessarily expensive; the optimum is usually to use them in a supporting role in conjunction with another approach.

When outside AI consultants are used it is better to employ two rather than one and indeed to use occasional days of others when needed. When two are employed to work together they can discuss ideas and develop them, so giving a better result. It need not cost much more to employ two since they can work in parallel on different areas and complete the work in a shorter time. It is only during discussions that both will work on a single problem, and this should result in better advice and a shorter period to examine each problem.

Standard method of using consultants

Each of the approaches described above has disadvantages. A combined approach has been found to be better. This is described in outline below.

After preliminary conversations with senior managers, a group of people is selected from the business to prepare a list of opportunities. The group generally includes a senior manager, department heads and one or two representatives of the DP department. This group works with the consultants used to identify opportunities in the business. The consultants explain the capabilities and limitations of AI to the group, giving illustrations of business uses. The group and the consultants together examine the business needs, constraints and operations. This is done methodically, rapidly and superficially and produces a long list of possible AI application areas. During this process the primary concern is to identify areas where machine intelligence might be beneficial if it could be built. Feasibility and cost are ignored at this stage.

Similarly, the group makes no effort to quantify benefits nor to define functional requirements. As each possible opportunity is identified, it is added to the

Identifying Opportunities

wish-list and the search is continued for another.

The above outline description is amplified below.

The initial discussions and decision to proceed are always conducted with, and taken at, a high level of management – directors, general managers or chairmen. The involvement of senior management at the outset is most important because systems which include AI can alter fundamental aspects of the business. Only senior management can decide whether or not to make such changes, and thus they must become involved at some stage. It is easier for them and saves wasted effort if they are in right at the beginning.

The preliminary is a two-hour presentation to the senior management on what AI is, how AI can be used to improve profitability, why stand-alone expert systems are often not as successful as is hoped and should include one or two examples. At the end of this meeting the managers decide whether or not to proceed and identify the group which is to conduct the study. The group usually includes the senior manager(s), departmental managers and often some business analysts from the data processing department. The group size is usually between six and twelve members.

The next step is to provide the group with a sufficient understanding of AI and its practical uses and to ensure that the consultants have an outline understanding of the business operation, its opportunities, constraints and threats. The time needed for this step varies between businesses. At one extreme it may be undertaken in a single morning with the whole group present. At the other, the business analysts/DP staff may spend two or three days with the AI development group during which they examine selected examples and explain the business to the consultants.

When this longer method is necessary the two or three days are often taken as half days over a week's duration giving sufficient time to assimilate the information. Once the analysts and the consultants have achieved an information level sufficient for communication, the whole group meets as before. However, as the analysts will have discussed possibilities with the consultants during the training period, the group starts with some possible areas already identified.

The initial meeting of the whole group should last a full day if this is at all possible. It has been found that progress is very slow for the first hour or so but speeds up as the first opportunities are identified and the group members learn what they are looking for. This effect is not so marked if the group adjourns and is then reconvened a few days later.

It is useful for the group meeting to follow an agenda which provides for the business to be examined by individual areas and also as a whole. The agenda can be based on the organisation's internal structure or on the flow of work through the organisation. Though the use of both methods would ensure that less is omitted, there is seldom sufficient justification for occupying the additional time of the managers which this would require. Where at the end of the meeting there are indications that several applications may have been omitted, the analysts may be asked to continue with the consultants and to report back at a second group meeting on any additions found. The group meeting is usually attended by two or three consultants who have experience with different types of AI technology and different business areas.

Businesses differ and both imagination and careful thought are necessary in combining AI and business know-how to match particular circumstances. The work required can, however, be reduced by following general guidelines which may help to identify some opportunities fairly easily. The opportunities sought are either to use AI in place of the current use of human intelligence or to achieve some currently unfulfilled goal.

Identifying Opportunities

These two categories of use require different approaches.

The first category comprises intelligent and possibly skilled work which is currently being performed by humans. It has not been performed by machine because until now the technology has not been (and in many cases is still not) available. By examining the tasks which humans perform, those opportunities should be identifiable. It would be possible to examine every job performed by humans within the business and so isolate all the internal opportunities for AI, but this would be an arduous and expensive task, certainly not one which could be completed by a small group within a few hours, since, as with the nostro reconciliation system described in Chapter 2, the benefit and opportunity may lie in a small but time-consuming part of some human's work. Fortunately there are methods of isolating the most fruitful fields.

One method which is particularly useful in businesses which are extensive users of computer systems is to examine the work performed by humans which is adjacent to an existing conventional system; that is, work which is done using computer-printed output, display screens, keyboards and so on. The systems analysts have probably extended the existing computer systems outwards through the business to those points where a human was essential and irreplaceable by conventional computer methods. Many of these points are there because there was a need for intelligence or knowledge, so they deserve special examination.

The documentation produced in support of computer systems often includes diagrams showing what printed output and screen displays are produced and who uses them. Input is also shown. These diagrams can be extracted, collated and used to locate points where an AI addition may be valuable. Note that humans are also sometimes required for reasons other than intelligence, such as mobility, authority and so on. Not all interfaces with conventional systems are associated with a need for intelligence.

A second method which incorporates several indicative factors is to try to identify classes of workers who for at least part of their job:

- are primarily sedentary
- don't spend much (work) effort talking to others either on the telephone or in person
- perform a repetitive decision-making function several times an hour
- can chat to each other or to visitors whilst working, without (much) loss of effectiveness
- are either numerous or are hard-pressed to complete their work on time.

When considering the work done by humans, whichever approach is used, remember those who are not in the business organisation but who are associated with it. Thus one should consider customers and their tasks as this can lead to the identification of additional or improved services which may be offered. Nearly all businesses can be improved by and can benefit from improvements to their customer's businesses. Similarly, there may be an advantage in identifying improvements which could be made by the businesses suppliers as they may be able to improve the service the business receives.

The second group of opportunities lies in those tasks which are not currently done either because it would be too expensive to use human intelligence, because human intelligence cannot produce the answers at the speed required, because the volume of information to be used is too high or because no one knows how to perform those tasks. These opportunities are represented by unsolved business problems or as constraints, and they are most obvious to senior managers and businessmen, which is one of the reasons why it is vital to

Identifying Opportunities

have such people in the group which meets to identify possible opportunities.

The authors have only one suggested means for eliciting these second-group items and that is to attempt to list a number of business wishes which start with 'If only . . .'. Most will be irrelevant at first sight, but many may reveal an opportunity when examined in detail. For example, 'If only we could reduce our inventory value' might suggest the use of intelligent software to examine the holding of each stock item against use or to adjust order and reorder size levels against an intelligent forecast of the future over the next period.

Once the wish-list is completed, each item on it is given a preliminary rating for feasibility, as explained in the next chapter. When AI consultants are available and the group has a full-day meeting, the last hour is usually reserved for the consultants to give to the group an 'off the cuff' feasibility assessment of each item.

The major cost of the exercise is, of course, the time of senior and departmental managers for a full day. The cost of employing the consultants is that of fees and expenses for somewhere between four and twelve man days; with fee rates at the time of writing, this is between £1750 and £5000. The number of possible applications on the wish-list can vary widely according to the business, but the average is probably around twenty.

Identifying opportunities without consultants

First, it is still important for senior management to be involved at an early stage. Where the suggestion to search for AI opportunities in the business comes from elsewhere in the organisation, the proposal should be sent to senior management and their backing and commitment secured. If this backing cannot be attained, then a second attempt should be made once a number of apparently feasible opportunities have been identified. It is seldom worth proceeding beyond this point without the presence of senior management backing. Successful AI systems suggest changes to the business, and it is often in these changes that the real profit lies. Such changes cannot be made unless senior management is willing to make them and feels comfortable with the approach.

After this initial preparation, the selected group meet as detailed in the preceding section, without, of course, the presence of consultants.

The meeting will become productive more rapidly if it can start by examining one or two possible opportunities in its own operations. This can be achieved by arranging for the business analysts who will attend the meeting to carry out a brief preliminary survey on their own for that purpose.

It is useful to have the meeting chaired by a facilitator rather than by the most senior manager present. The senior manager is there to contribute his specialised knowledge of the business and not in his normal role of controller and decision maker. If he takes the chair, part of his attention will be given to the control of the meeting rather than to contributing to it.

The chairman should take particular care to ensure that all possibilities which might benefit the business are accepted by the group and recorded, even those which are obviously infeasible to the point of absurdity. This is very important as those absurd ideas can often be divided into subsets, some of which may be both feasible and highly profitable.

A second advantage of an accepting attitude is that those group members who have thought of an idea but are reluctant to express it lest it be considered unsuitable or infeasible will do so more readily once a few 'wild' ideas have been tabled but not rejected.

Identifying Opportunities

Summary

The first step towards making effective use of AI techniques in a business is to prepare a 'long list' of possible opportunities without regard to their possible cost or feasibility. This list is best obtained by:

- acquiring the support of senior management
- establishing a group of between six and twelve people comprising:
    - a senior manager
    - department heads
    - one or two business analysts
    - AI experts if possible
- giving the group members a preliminary briefing
- allocating a full day to a group meeting
- searching systematically, particularly at the periphery of existing systems, for possible opportunities
- recording all suggestions that might be beneficial, even those which are obviously infeasible.

4 Assessing Feasibility

Once a list of AI opportunities has been prepared for the business, the next task is to identify those which can be constructed and to score each one according to the estimated difficulty, speed and cost of construction.

Some problems can be solved in several ways using different methods, and it can be difficult to know which to use. Some problems require one of the less well-known methods if they are to be solved at all. The ideal way of deciding how feasible a particular AI application may be is to have two or three AI practitioners from different specialist areas to contribute their opinions.

However, though it may be desirable to use experts, this is not always practical. They are in short supply and are difficuult to obtain. There are sensitive business situations which managers may prefer not to expose to someone outside the organisation. Thus it may be necessary for a business to estimate the feasibility of a possible intelligent application using only its own resources. Moreover, many managers like to have a general understanding of any subject which may make a significant difference to their profitability even when they intend to delegate the detail to experts. This chapter has been included in this book to give some guidance on how to assess the feasibility of a possible application.

In this chapter only those conditions which indicate 'easy to build', or 'using common techniques' are covered. The chapter can be used to identify applications which are feasible. It cannot be used to identify with

Assessing Feasibility

confidence those applications which are infeasible.

Another word of warning is necessary. During the detailed definition of the functions and operations of an AI system, the beautiful simplicity of the initial concept can disappear among exceptions, variations and so on. Usually a compromise can be found between either leaving all the hard parts to a human or making the system so complex that it is uneconomic to build. Usually, but not always, some tasks that appear at first sight to be feasible, even easy, turn out on further examination to be beyond present capability.

The contents of the chapter are arranged according to the type of intelligent system considered. As most intelligent business systems are expert systems, the next section gives some guidance on assessing the feasibility of a possible expert system from a consideration of the knowledge or expertise which it should incorporate. After this a summary is given of the conditions under which speech systems are practical. Robotics involves many considerations other than that of incorporating intelligence in a machine. These are outlined in the section which then follows, but the reader is advised to obtain an expert evaluation of feasibility for opportunities of this class. Creative systems are then mentioned, although we have said that, with the exception of learning systems, they are not currently feasible as a business proposition. The final section discusses implementation feasibility. It is sometimes possible to build a prototype which has the required functionality, only to find that it is very difficult to incorporate the same functions into existing systems.

Classes of knowledge or expertise

Expert systems are so called because not only are they perceived as 'intelligent' but they also incorporate some permanent knowledge or human expertise which they use in reaching a result. The amount, the nature of and the relationship between the items of knowledge which they will need in order to solve problems are useful indicators of:

- how feasible it will be to build an expert system
- the expert-system technology which will be needed.

Humans use very different kinds of knowledge in problem solving. Generally they do not know themselves how they do it, and frequently the way in which they believe and say they solve a particular class of problem is drastically wrong. In one application, for example, the senior 'expert' explained that his decision was primarily guided by one group of information and a second group was used occasionally as a check. Tests showed that the junior experts did not use the first group of information at all. It could be completely changed without influencing the decision reached – only the second group was used.

The senior expert, when told, was horrified to learn that his staff were reaching their decisions the wrong way. He demonstrated how it should be done, and his decision also proved independent of the first group, though he was quite sure that he used the first group to reach his decision and the second group only for verification.

This is a frequent occurrence, particularly when the decision is reached by a 'learned response' or similar process. Experts generally believe that they reach their decisions through a sequence of reasoned steps, whether or not they actually do so. If you ask a mathematician 'What is the product of 2 and 3?', he will say '6'. Ask how he reached that conclusion and he will never say 'Because I learned it by heart as an infant'. He will tell you how it could be proved from some elementary principles.

Assessing Feasibility

Scientific experts, including most AI workers, are particularly prone to believe that reasoning is the only means of reaching intelligent conclusions and that therefore the only satisfactory knowledge which should be included in an expert system is that which permits the construction of a reasoning process to derive a decision and a reasoned argument to support it.

There are situations where wholly logical step-by-step reasoning is ideal, but for this to be possible the knowledge must be sufficiently complete and interconnected to allow chains of reasoning to be built through it in any direction. AI workers refer to such bodies of knowledge as 'well-structured knowledge domains'. Knowledge of this kind is very common in the wake of man. For example, scientists like to classify things according to some logical structure and invent 'super classes' such as 'mammal' and 'canine' to enable them to produce reasoning chains in their work areas.

As a second example, man often defines rules such as those for obtaining supplementary benefit or for playing games which implicitly define a structure for successful operation. The spelling rules which were used in the example discussed in Chapter 2 are also of this type.

Where the knowledge is well structured, one can write down a set of rules which contain that knowledge. Thus a zoologist could write down a set of rules which identify mammals. Where it looks as though the knowledge needed for an application which could handle all cases could be written down like this without too much difficulty, a reasoning expert system is probably feasible. If it looks as though the rules should be written on two sheets of paper, it will be a small- to medium-sized system. If more than two are likely it will be of medium to large size. (One always needs more rules than appear to be required at first sight.)

If there are 'gaps' which prevent the formation of complete reasoning chains, or if a system which includes the complete knowledge is too expensive to develop or operate, then we must use partial knowledge. The subsequent methods used are not technically respectable; many AI workers would not consider that a system based on them could be classed as 'intelligent'. But they are effective and useful.

The most common of these non-reasoning techniques is the learned-response method which was mentioned earlier. In this a few pieces of trigger information are used to leap to a conclusion, which may be wrong, without any reasoning process between. Once a conclusion has been obtained there are usually provisions for checking whether it is 'reasonable' or not, and the method can be used in conjunction with a standard reasoning system which handles detailed refinement. For example, a mother may hear her child sneeze once and leap to the conclusion that he has a cold. She may be wrong; he could have spilled the pepper or have some obscure and very serious illness but because she is correct sufficiently often when she makes these leaps, she finds it a useful way of working. Once she has decided that the child has a cold, she checks her conclusion by taking his temperature.

There are many business situations where 'more often right than wrong' is better than nothing. If it is possible to define 'triggers' for the important conclusions the system should reach, then a learned response method is probably feasible. There is, however, one difficulty in using a learned-response technique. Since the approach is academically unacceptable, very little of the work done on it has ever been published. Thus the system builders may have trouble finding out how to construct an efficient learned-response system.

Voice and speech understanding

Word recognition systems recognise separately spoken words and can, for example, produce a typed display corresponding to those words. Speech understanding is the comprehension of what was meant from what has been said. Finally, voice synthesis systems produce spoken replies.

The current status of these three technologies is:

- word recognition: usable but not excellent
- understanding: very limited, usable in constrained situations only
- voice synthesis: good.

Word recognition is good where words are spoken one at a time, there are a limited number of words and the system can be taught the speech characteristics of its users. There are several business uses for this primitive activity. The control of a machine is an obvious application, but it can be used to allow travelling staff to ask questions of a computer over the telephone without their carrying special equipment. Thus a salesman might use such a system to obtain after-hours information on prices or delivery schedules. He would have to use a predefined word sequence such as 'Tell, pause, Product name, pause, Price', but the application would still be useful.

When words are spoken together as a sentence without clear gaps between them, the success rate falls. This may still be acceptable, particularly if the machine 'repeats back', since if it makes a mistake then the speaker knows and can give correction.

Where there may be a large number of unknown speakers, such as the general public, and they include men, women, children and a variety of accents, the system has either to store the details of every word to be recognised as spoken by representatives of all these groups or else it has to ask each new speaker to repeat a few standard words and so learn his voice characteristics. Speech details use a lot of store. When a 'speaker independent' operation is needed, the number of words to be recognised by the machine must be small.

If the proposed application can be implemented such that the computer will only need a vocabulary of about twenty words and the words can be spoken singly and the system can be taught the speech characteristics of those who will use it, then that application is feasible. The more 'extra' complexity one adds, the harder (or the more expensive) it becomes to build an effective system.

There is, however, a great deal of work being done in this field. A genuine word-recogniser which could handle a large vocabulary and had a reasonably low unit cost would drive a word processor from direct dictation and should have very large sales. This justifies extensive research into means of storing large vocabularies economically and will eventually result in the mass production of chips which will be suitable for special system use as well as for 'dictation to print' machines. If such machines are on the market as you read this, then far more will be feasible than has been suggested above.

Real comprehension of natural language as it is used by humans is still many years away, particularly for languages such as English, which allow wide variations in syntax. However, there are many special circumstances in which the subject matter of the conversation is constrained by the particular application to a narrow factual field, and in these a system may be able to deduce the meaning correctly most of the time. Fortunately most business needs are restricted in just this way. A system which could chat away on any subject would just waste time; one which can usually understand what is required of it, can check that it has understood correctly and can provide the appropriate response in its work area is not only more feasible, it is preferable.

Assessing Feasibility

Natural language understanding can sometimes be of use via a screen and keyboard but has most benefit when associated with a spoken-word recogniser and a synthesiser to give a system that will operate over a telephone or through a microphone and loudspeaker.

If the 'understanding' can be obtained through the recognition of a limited number of keyboards irrespective of their position in the sentence, then the application is probably feasible. If a restricted syntax and a constrained field of knowledge are possible, then a system is probably feasible.

Voice synthesis is now very good. It can be indistinguishable from human speech over a telephone and even fairly cheap systems are vastly better than the standard television programme 'robot voices'.

Robotics

Some robots are now commercially available; for example, intelligent machine tools such as paint sprayers. These can be examined prior to purchase and there is no difficulty in deciding whether or not they are feasible. There is only a problem when the opportunity requires the development of a new robot.

Robot devices incorporate not only the machine which moves but also appropriate sensors and a control system. The control system is usually an intelligent computer system which is connected both to the input sensors and to the motors which cause the machine to move. Overall feasibility depends on the feasibility of obtaining or building each of these parts and on other factors such as the safety aspects of the device.

Mechanical feasibility can be estimited by a mechanical engineer. Robots vary widely in complexity from very simple devices such as those which direct conveyed parts at switching points to very complex machines with many independently moving parts. Sometimes an existing machine can be adapted, although it may be difficult to equip it with intelligence because it does not have the sensors necessary for intelligent operation. Moreover, a machine which has an intelligent control of its movement cannot also follow a predefined movement sequence. At times its movements will be unexpected. This often causes safety problems when men and machines co-exist in the same place.

When it appears feasible to build a new machine or to adapt an existing one, the next task is to determine how feasible it is to provide the intelligent control. A good idea of that feasibility can be obtained by writing down the 'rules' which the machine should follow, just as though it were an expert system. A process engineer can usually make a good job of this task. In defining the rules, do not be surprised if additional sensors are found to be necessary.

If the opportunity still seems feasible, it is worth while asking a skilled roboticist to give an opinion. This is a difficult field; development costs can be high since one may need to develop prototype machines as well as computer systems, and expert advice is cheap by comparison.

Creative systems

There are four different classes of system which might be called creative. First there are those systems which apply a set of rules or knowledge in combination with input or random numbers to produce something which may be considered a 'creation'. Thus it is possible to define the rules of musical composition or the design of structures and obtain in the one case a score and in the other a girder design which have not been programmed into the machine. Such systems operate within the bounds set

Assessing Feasibility

when the knowledge was entered into them. They do not create new knowledge. They can be very useful, and they can also be highly feasible.

The second class are those systems which work with a human designer or other creative thinker to fill in details in his outline creation. These too are expert systems, similar in structure and limitations to the first class.

The third class, which is not yet practical, contains those systems which develop new solutions to problems. To do this one would need a system which is expert in the art of problem solving, and as yet there are none, though there have been some very interesting experimental attempts. The book *How to Solve It* by Polya (8) discusses this field intelligibly without going into any technical detail.

The fourth class comprises learning systems which improve with 'experience'. Fully automatic self-learning systems have a restricted scope as they are difficult to direct, but it is reasonably easy to build systems which work with a human partner who can add to the systems knowledge as he finds it necessary. When this is done the system improves and gives the human increasing support, including ready access to a computer memory. The man and the machine together can then continue to improve and can extend their joint ability beyond that previously possible.

Though these learning systems may not sound very likely, they are actually often feasible. They have an added benefit in that as the knowledge is built up slowly over a period, an organisation which installs one before a competitor will almost certainly stay in the lead till both become static. There is another benefit in that the knowledge is stored in the machine and is not transferred if the employee leaves and joins another firm. When a key employee leaves there is a period of inefficiency till his replacement is appointed and another whilst he is learning his new job. These two periods may last in total for several months, during which time the cost of errors may be high. Where the knowledge is held by a machine the savings can be large.

Design feasibility

Even when the functions required can be built, the system is not necessarily effective. For example, it may not be able to handle the necessary through-put, give the results when they are required or connect into existing systems which hold the information needed.

The hardware and languages which are ideal for building intelligent systems are often unsuited to business operations, however good they may be for research purposes when volumes are small. This is, no doubt, a temporary failing, but at present it is often necessary to build intelligent business systems in languages which are not well suited to the work in order to get the through-put and communication with other systems. When a system is built using unsuitable tools, it costs more to build and to maintain. A system which appears to be a practical proposition may cease to be cost-effective when implemented in its working environment.

As a general rule of thumb, very small high-through-put systems, small systems with medium demands for through-put and response time and large systems with small through-put (such as the stand-alone expert systems) can be implemented without excessive effort. When the system is large and through-put must be high there will be difficulties if the languages and tools available do not suit the details of the operation. A software engineer should be able to advise on this.

Assessing Feasibility 55

Summary

There are now many different methods of building intelligent systems. The advice in this chapter can help to identify opportunities which are probably feasible, but it *cannot* be used to identify those which are not.

Expert systems are probably feasible when either one or both of the following can be done:

- a set of rules could be written down on two sheets of paper
- a set of 'triggers' can be defined for the main conclusions.

Word recognition is feasible if you have a small vocabulary and a limited number of speakers or time to learn a speaker's voice characteristics. Continuous speech is borderline. Speech understanding is very limited but can nevertheless be useful.

Robots are expensive to develop; get an opinion from an expert before starting.

True creative systems are not feasible but some expert systems give the effect of creativity. A man and intelligent machine working together can sometimes find solutions to tasks which the man alone could not. Implementation in the live business environment may be difficult for large systems which require a high through-put and rapid response. Obtain advice from a software designer.

5 Preparing a Short List

The two previous chapters advised on the identification of a 'long list' of AI opportunity areas and gave guidance on assessing their feasibility. The next task is to decide which, if any, of those opportunities justify implementation.

The task is not easy. It is likely that all or most of the AI opportunities which have been identified are capable of improving profitability. Clearly the objective is to implement those applications where the probable net gain from a completed working system is significantly greater than the costs and risks involved in its development. The snag, as usual, is that it is easier to know the basis on which a decision should be made than it is to obtain sufficiently reliable cost and benefit forecasts to make the decision. The approach suggested in this chapter obtains improved forecasts and firmly controls investigative expenditure.

In organisations where AI is already accepted, each opportunity is judged on its own merits, and the method described later for preparing a short list does not apply.

Where AI technology is a novelty and there is no relevant experience available within the business one naturally limits the number of simultaneous AI implementations. Lessons learned on the first projects can be applied to later ones; there is then at least a chance that mistakes will not be repeated. The early projects should, moreover, be low cost and of short duration to limit the risk and to allow an early evaluation of both the profit-

Preparing a Short List

ability and the development method and controls. The short listing suggested in this chapter is to achieve these ends. Those opportunities which are excluded from the initial short list will not necessarily be either infeasible or unprofitable; some among them may indeed be excellent investments which can be safely implemented once the initial selection has proved its worth.

So retain the full list of identified opportunities. Regard the short list as a selection for a first phase or pilot rather than as a complete list of those opportunities which will be implemented.

Though the initial short list should consist of implementations which are of low cost and of short duration, they should also make a significant improvement to profitability. This is very important. There have been so many 'toy' AI systems built for business use that a marginally profitable AI implementation will do nothing to achive credibility and to encourage investment in other, more ambitious implementations, even though it is cost justified.

In summary, the steps proposed are as follows:

- Produce an initial short list by picking those applications which appear to be both feasible and profitable. The emphasis should be on feasibility, though profitability should not be neglected.
- Examine the consequences to the business if the application is successful. What else could usefully be changed to take full advantage of the added facility?
- Reassess the benefits likely to accrue from all the changes considered and review each possible application to determine whether there is sufficient potential to justify a more detailed investigation.
- Undertake sufficient problem identification and design detailing to determine the feasibility with a high level of confidence. This usually causes some changes as well as additions to the original concept.

- Determine whether the detailed work has invalidated the cost benefit estimates made previously. Review and decide whether to proceed to implementation.

These steps are expanded in the following sections.

Initial short listing

Although both feasibility and profitability are important, give priority to feasibility when making your initial selection. The short list should include two or three more items than the number intended for initial implementation. Most businesses start with two implementations since the results from one can be unrepresentative. When this policy is adopted, the short list should contain four or five items.

The first step is usually to 'score' each opportunity according to the value of its successful implementation. This is much easier and quicker than trying to attach financial benefits to each item. Moreover, since the next step is likely to change the scope of each short-listed opportunity, any sizeable effort spent in valuation would be wasted.

The second step is to obtain a view of how feasible it will be to implement each item. If expert assistance is available, use it here. If you can have your list reviewed by a panel of experts with different backgrounds and skills, then do so. If no assistance is available, then use the guidance contained in Chapter 4, supplemented if possible by a little reading selected from the References and Further Reading sections at the end of this book.

The short list should be selected from those with high feasibility and a good value score. Stay clear of the longer more complex items at first.

Redefining the requirement

If you consider the example explained in detail in Chapter 2 you will remember that the inclusion of a little bit of intelligent software in the conventional system changed the whole nature of the operation. The multiple printed listings which were the back-bone of the previous method became secondary and the work of the reconciliation clerks altered. They required different support and it became possible to give them better and different facilities; for example, to control actions and priorities.

It is never easy to work out all the consequences and opportunities which can follow from having intelligent software, but it is worth spending some time in doing it. There are usually two different aspects to consider. The first is to try to hit the optimum balance between human and machine intelligence so that the machine intelligence is kept as simple and as easy to implement as possible but with humans only needed to handle the minimum volume of difficult cases.

The second aspect is the impact on the conventional part of the system. What will now be necessary? What can be cut out and what can be usefully added? This demands imagination and a knowledge of the business. AI experts may not have the business experience necessary to do this job properly and often miss it out altogether. A good business analyst may make a better job.

Whatever method is adopted, the manager should make sure that the consequences and resultant opportunities have been fully thought through and that the changes suggested make good business sense.

Second review

The next step is more costly than those discussed so far. Previous steps will have involved a few man-days of work for each candidate opportunity; the next will require somewhere between twenty and fifty man-days. If the requirement has been redefined as suggested above, the likely benefits will have changed. Quite possibly the function of the AI software as stated in the initial proposal will have been cut back to make it smaller and simpler. The preliminary cost–benefit evaluation will thus need revision.

It is true that the changes should have been made to improve the return and to reduce the investment, but it can and sometimes does happen that more careful examination reveals unexpected difficulties. Technicians are often satisfied that they have a solution to a problem; they don't always appreciate that the solution must be cost-effective if it is to be of any practical value. Thus management may not get a full picture of the results of those changes unless they ask specifically for a valuation report.

If five opportunities are being examined concurrently, bring all five up to this second review stage, then select the best two, provided of course that they still appear to have sufficient potential to justify a more detailed examination.

Feasibility verification

This is a difficult activity to control. One is only absolutely certain that a system can be built when it has been built and found to work satisfactorily. Even then it is always possible to add to it. Expert systems in particular are prone to creeping expansion as more and more expertise is built into them. They are never complete; they have to be stopped.

At this point one needs reasonable confidence that a system can be built, an estimate of how long it will take and of how much it will cost, rather than a working system. Technical staff find it particularly difficult to make these judgements, especially when they have no previous experience of AI systems and so they are likely to go into too much detail. They will certainly do so unless they are reassured that management understands that they cannot give an authoritative answer without extensive research and that an opinion (which might be wrong) is all that is required.

The research needed at this stage is a combination of a study of available technology and a study of the problem. Where the opportunity is an expert assistant much of the work will be an initial attempt at defining the rule base. This may be done by building a prototype in an AI langauge, but it is usually sufficient to try to write down a set of rules in plain English. One should not aim to produce a complete working set of precisely defined rules; a partial set which covers the main cases is sufficient to prove feasibility.

During this process the 'requirement' is often amended yet again as work reveals that some parts which originally looked difficult are actually simple and *vice versa*.

Benefit verification

When the technicians are reasonably confident that they can build an adequate system, reassess the benefits and this time use values. The next step may be to proceed to implementation, having made sure that the benefits from that implementation will exist.

Go or no-go decision

There is no clear demarcation between the activities discussed above and those described in the next chapter as the initial part of the development process. This is natural enough; the same can be said of conventional software and indeed of almost any process which is primarily one of problem definition and design. The two tasks are seldom clearly separable. Design work reveals the need for greater detail in the problem definition which, once completed, enables further design leading to another iteration of the two tasks.

Continual iteration is fine technically but does not facilitate the control needed to prevent development continuing indefinitely. A formal review is recommended at this point. The likely benefits and costs should be considered and a decision made on whether or not this opportunity should proceed into development. If it is to proceed then it should do so with clearly defined and agreed objectives and with cost and time budgets. There will be changes and variations made during the development; it is even possible that unforeseen problems will cause the project to be abandoned; but these are the standard objections which can be proffered when controls are imposed whatever the nature of the work. AI systems are no different from ordinary systems in this respect, except in degree. They are more difficult to define accurately before development starts, and thus they tend to change more during development. This should mean that their justification is sufficient to cover a larger percentage contingency, not that they cannot or should not be properly controlled.

The go or no-go decision should be formal. It should include evaluations by the experts or users of the expected benefits and by the technicians of the probable costs and feasibility risks, and a development plan if the technicians consider that development is feasible. It is

Preparing a Short List 63

best to ask for a written briefing followed by a review meeting rather than to rely on written briefings alone, since when a new technology is introduced into a business written communication on it is never fully effective.

Summary

When AI has not previously been used successfully within a business it is best to start by implementing two applications which are likely to be:

- quick to build, simple and with a low risk of failure
- significantly profitable.

These two applications should be selected from the 'long list' of possible opportunities by an iterative process in which confidence levels in the two aspects of feasibility and profitability are improved at each step. The steps suggested are:

- Select those five opportunities which at first sight appear to comply most closely with the selection criteria.
- For each of the five, consider what the side-effect opportunities and changes to the business may be and whether the AI task can be simplified.
- Review all five, rating their profitability and feasibility as now seen using a simple scoring system. Select the best two for more detailed assessment.
- For these two opportunities, undertake sufficient work (but no more than that) to be reasonably confident that the AI system could be built and to obtain an estimate of the method, cost and time that would be used. Obtain an approximate value of the likely benefit.
- Undertake a formal review of the two selected opportunities and make a go or no-go decision.

Allow for unforeseen cost increases which are likely when new technology is first used in a business. If the decision is 'Go' then establish clear goals and budgets. If the decision is 'No-go' then bring forward another of the initial five to this point.

6 Development and Implementation

AI is implemented, through computer software and stored information, on computer hardware. The development and implementation of an intelligent system has much in common with the development and implementation of a conventional system, and in general the same problems will be met and the same management methods can be used to solve or to contain these problems. A general familiarity with conventional software projects has been assumed and the common areas have been taken for granted.

Although much is similar, there are of course differences. These differences must be recognised and reflected in the controls used if a cost-effective implementation of an intelligent subsystem is to be achieved. This chapter explains the nature of these differences, discusses the principle management problems that they create and finally suggests variations to the normal controls used on conventional software projects to make them better suited to intelligent software projects.

Underlying differences

There are two chief differences between conventional and intelligent software developments which underlie the special peculiarities and problems of intelligent software projects. The first important difference lies in the significant extension of functionality which is involved in the use of AI. Conventional software has already changed from the early systems of the 1960s, which were in general pure replacements for existing manual systems, to the modern complex systems, which almost invariably provide functions which were not previously available. It is easy to define what an exact replacement system should do. It is very much harder to define the requirements of an extended-function system.

The provision of an additional function within a system alters the capability and nature of that system. This will change the environment within which that system operates – if it does not, the additional function is of no value. For example, if management information is improved, then management action will change. As it becomes easier to pinpoint exceptional or unsatisfactory items or to identify opportunities, managers will concentrate their attention on smaller areas and in so doing will alter their usage of and demand for other information. It is for this reason that the requirement specification of a modern conventional system is difficult to define.

The twin questions of 'What should this system do?' and 'What will be the consequences if it does that?' iterate by discussion or by prototyping, and there is no completely correct means of deciding what the system should do.

Intelligent systems extend this process even further. Managers have learned how difficult it can be to obtain a satisfactory requirement specification for a modern conventional system and reluctantly expect and allow for the inevitable delays and discussions. Intelligent systems are more capable than conventional systems, and in consequence it is even more difficult to decide what they are required to do.

There is a further closely related problem with intelligent systems in that one needs to define the intelligence

Development and Implementation

and knowledge which they should use in their work. Clearly one cannot attempt to provide them with the vast intelligence, experience and knowledge of a human. The aim is to provide only that which is needed to achieve their purpose. When a conventional system is defined one needs to know 'how it should be done'. When an intelligent system is defined one needs to know 'how an intelligent human would do it'. This is a much harder task. The methods are not written down, one has to ask and it is commonplace to find that the way experts actually work is different from the ways in which they think they work.

There have been several experiments in which experts were asked what information they used to solve a problem. Then they were given test problems in which the information they claimed to rely on had been falsified, and they still achieved a correct solution. Yet when information which they stated to be almost irrelevant was falsified they got the the answer wrong. It takes longer than one would expect to obtain a working version of the intelligence and expertise that will effectively solve problems, and usually two or three attempts are needed to do so.

The second significant difference between the development of conventional and intelligent systems is the difference in the quality of the constructional tools available. Over the past thirty years the tools available to build conventional systems have been extended, developed and refined. Programs can be generated efficiently, errors can be tracked down, data storage is handled by powerful multi-purpose handlers and so on. By contrast, the tools which can be used to build intelligent systems are much less developed and many are unusable in the typical business environment since they cannot handle the necessary through-put. Intelligent subsystems may have to be built, at least in part, the hard way. Also, intelligent software. This is only a temporary problem; the tools are on the way, but as yet they are not available.

Design or evolve?

The first difference in managing the development of an intelligent subsystem is in the criteria used to decide whether to design the software or to let it evolve. We have seen that it is difficult to establish what intelligent software should do and should contain, which suggests that evolution is desirable, at least as a means of defining functionality and content. Prototyping is now well established as a means of deciding the functionality of conventional systems, and it is common practice to produce a prototype and try out variations and alternatives before building an operational version.

Intelligent systems and, in particular, expert systems are always evolutionary. The normal stand-alone consultant system is built initially with a small number of basic rules, which are adjusted and added to over the whole life of the system. The concepts of 'versions' and 'releases' are not used, and the system changes from day to day. Though this is an effective means of building good expert-system prototypes, it is not satisfactory for live systems since it lacks control, does not facilitate effficient operation and can lead to unexpected 'behavioural problems' when rules are changed or added. This does not mean that a prototype cannot evolve while the live system remains static; indeed, this is an ideal strategy.

An operational intelligent system which is contributing to a business cannot have the same evolutionary freedom as it could in a research situation. We do not want a system which can be altered easily by its users; indeed, it is frequently essential that it be protected from them. Moreover, an intelligent system can make heavy

Development and Implementation

demands on computer resources, particularly when handling a large through-put. The original system and any later additions must be so constructed as to handle the processing in an efficient manner. The operational intelligent system must therefore be purpose-designed rather than evolved.

It is generally best, therefore, to start the development by using an evolutionary prototype and to use this to define what the initial operational version should be. Once the prototype is giving adequate results, an operational version can be designed and built. With conventional systems the prototype is discarded at this point since further changes are not expected. However, where intelligent systems are in use it is better to retain the prototype and to use it to investigate the value and practicality of possible changes which are suggested during the operational life of the live version. The prototype can thus continue to evolve until a new operational version is clearly justified. A new version is then designed and built or the design of the previous version is modified to update it to the current status of the prototype. This method gives the benefits of evolution without the risks resulting from continual change to the live system.

Stopping the prototype

The prototype of an intelligent system evolves. Each change incorporates new facilities, knowledge and so on proposed by the users and in turn suggests new changes which can improve it further. The process is continuous and there is no stage at which the users and the technicians can see a clear break-point. When a consultant expert system is being constructed the period of continuing improvement can last for four or five years, possibly even longer.

The prototype of an assistant expert system will, if left unchecked, tend to grow in expertise and intelligence in just the same way till it is no longer just an assistant. Similarly, other forms of intelligent system will evolve. This continuing growth may be valuable, but it does not encourage the early implementation of a useful operational system. This will only be achieved if management monitors progress and identifies the point at which the prototype is sufficiently developed to allow a cost-effective live implementation and then insists on that live version being implemented.

Both the users and the technicians will object. Improvements are about to be made. It would be better to wait just a little longer. Unless one expects this, those arguments can be very convincing. The result is a series of delays until eventually the manager realises what is happening.

Once the live version is under way it can of course suffer the same fate as the prototype. A continuing stream of amendments will be suggested, all perhaps for good reasons, which ensure that the design task is so plagued by change that it is never completed. There may be some essential changes which have to be made; but avoid improvements – they can go on for ever.

A useful means of containing growth and concentrating the development group's attention on the live version is to insist on the production of an initial operational version but with the proviso that the group may thereafter present a plan to continue work on the prototype once the live version is in operational use. The various ideas for improvement are then not seen to be condemned. Indeed, they will not be condemned if they are sufficiently beneficial to justify the later development of a second live version. Moreover, the development team will be highly motivated to complete the live version in such a way as to prove effectiveness of their previous work, and they will do this as rapidly as they can

Development and Implementation

to allow them to return to the development of their improved prototype.

Once the live version is operational, any further work on the prototype should have proper justification. The development team will have learned much on the first development and will be a scarce resource within the business. They will be competent to undertake implementation of another intelligent application, and it may be more effective to use them on a new project than to continue with improvements to the current work.

System design

The design of an intelligent system is purely technical and it would be inappropriate to discuss technical problems in detail here. However, the system designers may have difficulty in converting a working prototype into an efficient design, and management should be aware of those difficulties and of the resources that may be needed to overcome them.

The prototype will probably have been constructed using AI tools. The live version may not be able to use those tools, or may not be able to use them throughout. Where this is the case the designer has to supply both the functionality of the prototype program and also the functionality incorporated in the tool which is used by the prototype program. AI tools incorporate software functions which do not occur in conventional software. A good designer can find difficulty in providing similar functions unless he knows the methods which have been developed by AI tool builders for building them. He may not even be aware that there are semi-standard methods which he can use.

His design is likely to be completed more quickly, be cheaper and easier to implement and less liable to error if he is given the opportunity to learn something about the designs which have been found to be effective.

The authors know of no training courses which are ideal for this purpose. The literature is very extensive and it is difficult for a newcomer to know what to look for or where to look for it unless he has a guide of some kind. When the implementation is being undertaken without assistance from an AI expert who can direct the designer to relevant papers, the designer should examine the design of the tool used to build the prototype. This will at least cover all the areas that may be needed and can indicate what subjects may warrant further investigation through a library search. The publications listed at the end of this book may be helpful.

One advantage of this approach is that the designer can be allowed a week or two of reading in parallel with the development of the prototype before he needs to start work on the design.

A second difficulty the designer may face is that of translating the prototype design into an efficient system. For example, when implementing an assistant expert system it may be necessary to implement some of the rules in conventional software to achieve the throughput and response which is required. Very little has yet been published on this subject; the technical references in the References and Further Reading sections at the end of this book may help, but the designer may have to devise his own method of solving the problem. Often the results are better and more quickly attained when two designers work together – so allow some time for additional consultation.

Finally, where the intelligent system is an expert assistant, there will be a need for the system to explain how it arrived at its results to its human partner. That explanation must be both brief and clear; often a verbal explanation would take too long to assimilate, and some symbolic or graphic means of explanation is necessary. Someone with experience in the design of modern

Development and Implementation

human/computer interfaces can be very helpful. If possible, allow the designer to have a day or two of expert advice.

Software construction

The software should be built using any good method which meets the design needs. The normal rules of good practice such as modular design all apply as for conventional software.

When a conventional language or generator is to be used, there should be no need for special training of any kind. However, if the system is to be built using one of the AI object-oriented languages, then training will almost certainly be required. They are very different from conventional languages at a conceptual level and familiarity with the one does not help in knowing how to use the other.

Testing

No conventional software system can be 100 per cent tested. There are too many possible combinations of input and stored data to test them all. However, there are methods of testing in common use which will find enough errors to assure a system quality which is adequate for its purpose and reasonably reliable. These methods test the software on two bases. One basis is that of required functionality and is intended to find out whether the system behaves as it should behave. The other basis is the system structure; the logical paths within the system are identified and each path is tested in turn.

With intelligent software there is often no clearly defined permanent physical paths which the system will follow. The route through the software is decided by the data as before, but the software decides which route is appropriate. One cannot always draw a software map of an intelligent system and be certain that all paths are represented on it. Thus one of the two normal methods of defining tests is unreliable or infeasible. The methods used to test conventional systems test the program, they do not test the data. Even when the system uses conversion tables or other permanent data which will remain constant for the full life of the system, one would not normally apply tests to every value in those tables. There is a significant structural difference in the two types of system which has a strong influence on testing strategies. There is a close interrelationship between the rule table of an expert system and the software. The rule table *is* the system; the software is just a device for manipulating it. The rule table should therefore be tested.

Intelligent systems, since they are more capable than conventional ones, are harder to test and require more tests to achieve any given level of confidence in their performance. Less is known about how to test them efficiently. Management actions that derive from this are:

- Ensure that testing prior to implementation is more extensive than usual.
- Expect a higher probability of error in the live system when it is first implemented. If an error can have serious consequences, do not rely on the system operating correctly when it is first installed. Use an extended period of parallel running or caution the human 'partners' to be critical rather than to passively accept its every response.

Post-implementation growth

In discussing prototyping earlier in this chapter, the retention of the prototype was recommended as being a useful means of exploring post-implementation changes. Changes may be desirable:

- to correct an error found in the live system
- to update the system to meet changes in its environment
- to extend the capability of the system and so increase its functionality and work load.

Errors can survive undetected in any software, particularly those which only appear under very unusual conditions. Most errors which reach the live system are however detected during the initial period of operation, and nearly all changes in the immediate post-implementation period are intended to correct errors. Environmental change can occur at any time, and system changes for this purpose may be required throughout the system life. Once it is clear what change to the system behaviour is desired the next task is to decide how to make that change. If a particular change is made inside the system, will the system performance actually become the one that is desired? A prototype can be used to answer such questions without the need to experiment on the live version, whether the system be conventional or intelligent.

The chief difference lies in the possibility of extending the capability of the system. An expert system can often be extended such that it becomes capable of handling conditions which were previously beyond its ability and which it passed to its human partner. Such extension can become desirable as through-puts increase, as the business grows or as the feasibility of using the system becomes better understood. Extension can become possible as, through regular contact with an intelligent system, the users gain a better understanding of the methods which they use to resolve those cases which are beyond the system's capability. Thus many, probably the majority, of expert systems are able to evolve into something more useful.

It is valuable to review live intelligent systems at intervals and to decide whether further extensions might be both beneficial and feasible. When this appears to be the case the existence of a prototype facilitates the initial stages of development.

Controls

Control over an intelligent system development should reflect the changes which occur in the nature of the work as development proceeds.

The initial stage incorporates a high research content as work progresses towards defining what the system should do and how it should do it. Planning and estimating are both essential and difficult. Plans require frequent revision and both overruns and underruns are to be expected. During this phase, control is best exercised by close managerial contact with the work and constant monitoring to decide when a point has been reached where the development of a live version should begin or, alternatively, that the work should stop and the project be abandoned.

Once development of the live version is commenced, the project should be controlled exactly as if it were a conventional project. The only difference is that if the development staff are not experienced in building AI systems, as is probably the case, they may run into difficulty or take longer than they expected to complete the development. For these reasons management should provide an extended contingency against estimation error.

Development and Implementation

Summary

It is difficult to define exactly what an intelligent system should do or how it should be constructed. The initial construction of an experimental prototype is recommended. The prototype should be developed until it gives satisfactory results.

At this point further development of the prototype should be resisted, but the prototype should be retained. The design of a live version should be commenced against a frozen specification which is defined by the prototype. The designer should be given the opportunity to learn something of the way in which intelligent systems have previously been constructed. He should be given support from another designer towards building a system which is efficient and given assistance with the design of an effective human/computer interface. Design will take rather longer than the design of a conventional system.

The software can be built using any method which is appropriate to the design. If no intelligent system tool is used, the software can be built exactly as though it were a conventional system, and the construction staff will need no special training. If a tool is used, then construction staff should be taught how to use it and how it works.

Testing will need more effort than would be required if the system were conventional. Errors may survive into the live version, so an extended period of parallel use is desirable. The system should be reviewed at intervals to decide if further development, initially on the prototype, might be profitable.

The controls applied should differ at different stages of the process. The first phase should be controlled primarily by close regular contact between the development team and the supervisory manager. The construction of the live version should be controlled as if it were a conventional software project.

7 AI and the Small Business

Though the needs of a small business may be identical in principle to those of a large one, differences of scale make significant changes to the cost-effectiveness of intelligent applications. First, the manager can make a larger proportion of the necessary decisions himself; the ratio of human intelligence to business volume and complexity is higher, and thus there is less benefit in using AI. Second, the business volume from which any investment must be recovered is lower. Purpose-built software is expensive, and its cost is practically independent of volume, thus only the most rewarding applications, if purpose-built, will give an adequate return.

This does not mean that intelligent systems cannot be effective in small businesses, only that the selection of applications and the means of procurement will differ. The small business can seldom afford to obtain a competitive edge by having the sole version of a system, but it can afford to adopt an existing system and perhaps to add to the facilities which it provides. The reason that small businesses can use an existing system is that they generally operate in localised markets. It is sufficient to have an advantage over the competition in that market; there is no need for concern that others elsewhere have the same advantage.

The advice contained in the previous chapters is relevant, but subject to some adaptation. The example used in Chapter 2 to support the argument that AI techniques can improve profitability is still valid, but, of course, the

AI and the Small Business

application is not likely to be cost-justified since reconciliation work will probably be trivial. Chapters 3 to 5 can be used to identify those opportunities which are desirable, but since a small business is unlikely to build its own systems, that information will be used to determine whether or not to pressurise a supplier or trade association to provide what is needed or to select a package rather than to decide what to build.

Chapter 6, which discusses the construction of intelligent systems, may be of service if it is decided to add to or to adapt a bought-in package. Design for high through-put will be less relevant, and it may not be necessary to stop growth at a suitable point since an evolutionary prototype may be used as the live operational system. However, it will be even more vital to ensure that time and money are not wasted in adding frills.

Some of the examples in Part II will be of particular interest. For instance, in Chapter 8 (on sales and order processing) there is a brief discussion about the ways in which a distributor or wholesaler can provide an improved service to the retail outlets which he serves. That discussion may assist a retailer to evaluate the services which he is offered but could also indicate a possible personal computer application which could be owned and developed by the retail business. However, even though much of the contents of this book has a bearing on the needs of small businesses, they do have special problems in obtaining suitable systems. This chapter addresses some of those problems and suggests means of solving them.

Packages

There are a number of shells (expert systems packages without a rule base) on the market. They each have different advantages and disadvantages, and they are seldom appropriate for the high-through-put embedded systems which are of most use to large businesses. They can be useful, however, where the volumes are lower and where only a few rules are needed. Some software houses have started to use shells to build packaged solutions to general problems. The purchases may have to add special information to the standard set of rules in order to tailor them to their own specific needs, but a package will include guidance on how to make those additions.

Although there are as yet very few such packages on the market, more can be expected in the near future. These will no doubt be advertised in the appropriate trade press. When deciding whether or not a particular intelligent package will meet the need, take all the usual precautions just as though it were a conventional package.

Do-it-yourself

Many small businesses have had special systems built in BASIC or a similar conventional language. When the system is small the results of this approach can be quite satisfactory and the costs are minor. It is possible to have small special-purpose intelligent systems built in the same way. There are two points to watch out for it you decide to try this. First, it is often very difficult to find out what rules should be included in the system. Even a small task where an English-language version of the rules can be produced without effort can prove troublesome when those rules have to be stated formally. Second, an intelligent system which omits a few crucial rules can give excellent results under certain conditions and very poor results at other times.

So, if you try this approach, make sure your system

AI and the Small Business

builder has some understanding of AI; allow him plenty of time to state the rules. Treat the results of the system with great caution until it has been tested under as many different conditions as possible.

Summary

Intelligent systems can be beneficial to small businesses, though not to the same degree as they can be to large ones. Package solutions are now just coming onto the market, but they should be carefully evaluated. A do-it-yourself system can be effective provided that whoever implements it has appropriate training.

PART II
AI IN ACTION

Introduction to Part II

The first part of this book includes a description of a method for identifying suitable areas of a business in which AI might prove a cost-effective addition. It is, however, quite difficult advice to follow unless one has first some idea of the sort of applications which may be suitable. The single case study in Chapter 2 demonstrates that there are such applications but, on its own, does not help much in finding others. One needs several examples to gain a proper understanding. This part of the book discusses possible applications of AI technology in thirteen common business activities. The purpose of this is to enable readers to develop their understanding and so help them to identify real opportunities in their businesses.

The authors have attempted to include a sufficiently wide range of business activities so that the majority of readers will find something which relates to their particular business.

The reader is asked to bear the following points in mind when reading the remaining thirteen chapters:

- Businesses vary widely, and a task which is apparently common to several will usually prove to differ significantly in detail and in importance when examined more thoroughly. Thus a task where an intelligent element is a cost-effective addition in one business may be inappropriate to another. With any list of examples there is certain to be some which are irrelevant or unsuited to each reader's business, and

for some readers there may be none in the list which is appropriate.
- The authors are employees of a company which assists clients to identify and to implement commercially profitable AI. In such instances it would be unethical to describe identifiable implementations, and in some cases this can involve completely avoiding any mention of particular application areas. Some applications have been excluded from discussion for this reason. The omission of a particular application from discussion should not be interpreted therefore as implying that an AI solution would necessarily lack feasibility or be unprofitable.
- The illustrations can be of use in learning how to identify opportunities; they should not be used as checklists.
- The following chapters are all independent of one another. They need not be read in the order in which they have been collated, nor indeed is it necessary to read them all.

The authors are not themselves experts in all business areas; when working on a problem they rely on their client's expertise in that area. There are also areas in which they have no direct experience on which to draw, and in these they are dependent on reports from others. Thus there was a choice to be made between offering a wide selection of illustrations with an associated risk of error and providing a smaller but safe selection.

Though care has been taken to verify terminology and the discussion in these chapters, they may contain undetected errors. Corrections and suggestions will be gratefully received and applied to improve any future editions.

8 Sales and Order Entry

The principal objective of most order-capture support systems is to maximise revenue by increasing the value of each order placed to the limit of the customer's credit. The ideal is to maximise profit from the available revenue, considering the costs as well as the price associated with each product. This is difficult to achieve since one needs to know both what costs to attach to each line and also the means of including costs in the salesman's objectives. The nearest that most organisations get to this goal is to push specific items where sales are particularly desirable. The choice of those items is frequently restricted to new products, advertised products and to items which are overstocked, deteriorating or are about to be replaced.

Since, in the longer term, customer satisfaction determines order value, a subsidiary objective is to achieve a service which buyers perceive as being of at least a satisfactory quality. Order-capture support systems must ensure that customers have the right goods delivered and that all (or most) sales promises are fulfilled.

Finally there is the secondary objective of minimising the costs of taking and of fulfilling orders.

The following sections discuss possible AI tasks associated with each of these objectives.

The order-taking process

Orders can be prepared in three different ways. They may be:

- produced by the customer and posted in
- completed by a travelling salesman at the customer's site
- placed during a telephone conversation.

In the first case the supplier's influence over the order content is very restricted and little can be done to increase order value. When orders are taken by a travelling salesman or over the phone there are opportunities to increase sales by persuading the customer to add extra items to the order which that customer does not normally purchase or which he has forgotten to replenish and to increase the quantity of each item ordered.

In order to ensure that the customer has remembered to replenish his stocks of all those items which he normally buys, the salesman studies previous orders and may check the customer's remaining stock of each item. When this is not practical he tries to deduce the likely stock level. He does this by examining previous purchases from which he assesses the probable rate of consumption and so estimates the likely amount remaining in stock from the previous order. He then bases his suggestions as to what else the customer may need on those estimates. It is reasonably simple to do this when there is plenty of time. Consumption rates can be estimated using the following:

- previous history
- consumption rates currently prevailing in similar outlets which have been exposed to similar conditions (advertising, trade levels, climate, etc.)
- reference to that particular customer's requirements at that time for related or similar items.

Sales and Order Entry

The calculation is simple, but it does take time to do by hand and it is practically impossible to achieve when in conversation, particularly on the telephone when the total period available is short.

Expert systems to increase income

A small expert-system module which monitors an order as it is built up can provide estimates of consumption, remaining stock and so on, and can draw the telephone salesman's attention to other lines which may need replenishment. An overnight computer process can provide printed estimates for travelling salesmen, though it cannot allow for quantities included in current orders.

A similar argument indicates the possible use of an expert system to identify additional items which may attract a particular customer using an analysis of those sales known to us and also from the utilisation rates of similar customers. Here the ability of an expert system to explain its recommendations is particularly valuable as it indicates what the salesman should tell the customer in order to convince him to buy. It can, for example, give case histories to a retailer of similar customers who achieve high sales of the items to be recommended. Such a system, by ensuring that the extra lines suggested are likely to be profitable to the customer and not just an *ad hoc* sales pitch, will increase his satisfaction with the service offered.

A variant of the above can be used where the lines sold are logically interconnected. For example, the purchase of bricks indicates the need for mortar, and the purchase of a window-frame indicates the need for glass.

The normal means by which the number of units ordered is increased is through the use of volume discounts. The salesman points out to the customer that an additional 'so many' units will secure an improved discount level. Discounts are necessary to the maintenance of a competitive price for larger orders, but they are not an ideal means of increasing volume. The next discount threshold may be so close that only a minor increase is required, or so distant that it is not attractive. A larger order can be achieved most easily by convincing the customer that he can use or sell additional units. An expert system which makes estimates of those lines which may need replenishment also estimates the likely demand. When the customer places an order which is below the estimate, the salesman can use the expert system reasoning to convince the customer that he should increase the volumes. In the long term the customer should find this to be a useful extra service which helps him to avoid selling out of an item but does not clutter his shelves with slow-moving items. Where this is achieved the result is more effective than the use of discount thresholds.

Maximising profitability

Though it would be better to influence order content to maximise profitability rather than income, this objective is seldom attempted, as it is difficult using manual and conventional computer systems to allocate costs to products and to direct the salesman correctly. The cost-allocation decisions needed to determine which products should be sold in preference to others involve complex accounting decisions and should incorporate volume information. For example, the unit production costs of further items which are batch-produced depends on the volume already required. If there is a partly allocated batch already planned and the number of additional items lies within the unallocated portion of that batch, their cost will reflect only the normal production costs. If, however, a new small batch is needed,

Sales and Order Entry

the full production set-up cost must be carried by that small number, and thus the unit production cost of those additional items may be high.

Similarly, there will be benefits in giving a low priority to an item which is using a resource that is presently scarce and which is constraining operations. Clearing shelf space by the sale of bulky items can avoid the need for remote warehousing of other lines. Where the costs of raw materials are volatile there can be advantages in increasing the quantity of products made using cheaper raw materials and decreasing the production of those whose raw materials are more expensive, particularly if this can be done without increasing the stockholding costs of finished goods.

In theory one could build a mathematical model which would incorporate all the various profitability determinants and use this to advise salesmen on what they should push, which order lines are best increased in volume, and so on. In practice such a model is usually either unworkably large or of usable size but of little value. In appropriate circumstances, however, an expert system can give advice in this area which is sufficiently accurate to improve profitability.

Improving service levels

Most of the work which can be undertaken to improve the customer's perception of the service he receives lies outside the order-entry support system and is discussed elsewhere. Earlier in this chapter we identified means of helping the customer to order items and quantities which will improve his own business performance. These are the most significant contributions which AI can make to perceived service in order-entry support.

There are, however, additional opportunities which are appropriate under specific conditions which deserve mention. First, it may be desirable to allocate priorities to orders so that if there is contention between orders, then the orders which are more important from the supplier's viewpoint are serviced at the expense of the others. An expert system can be used to assess the business importance of every order and thus to ensure that no important orders are given a low priority because the order taker did not appreciate their importance at the time the orders were placed or because he was not aware of all the circumstances. Order priority assessment would normally take into account the usual factors such as trade history, order size and the customer's stated need for urgency. It would also consider some factors which are more difficult to handle when using conventional software, such as whether he is a nominated strategic target account, whether and how often he has previously complained, whether he is known to have an alternative source and similar measures of business vulnerability.

Second, it may be desirable to monitor the quality of customer service provided. The subsystem which does this will not lie wholly within the order-entry field but will straddle the complete process from order, through delivery, to post-delivery support. It will need input from the order-entry operation which is similar to that used by the order priority system discussed above. The two operations can be combined so that the priority system passes on a summarised view of the business risks attached to each order.

Supporting systems

The expert system discussed above will need information which may not be readily available. To predict probable demand in one outlet through comparison with demand in other similar outlets one needs to classify outlets and

Sales and Order Entry

correlate use by product line with outlet class. In many businesses such demand will vary according to season, weather, level of advertising and other outside influences. Since it can be very time-consuming to carry out and to update such an analysis, a supporting system should be built for this work. The search for patterns and the correlation of actuals with patterns is best done by an AI subsystem; the AI subsystems then operate in pairs with one undertaking the research and investigative work and the other applying those results to specific cases.

Use as a sales aid

An expert system mounted on a portable computer which could be used jointly by a salesman and the customer during the build-up of an order might be an effective sales aid. If the system was easy to use and the advice given convincing to the customer and sufficiently accurate to improve his business, it could be a possible replacement for alternate visits of a travelling salesman or a means of increasing the customer's order frequency.

Summary

The following possible uses for small embedded expert systems have been discussed:
- identifying lines stocked by the customer, omitted from the current order but likely to require replenishment
- identifying lines not normally taken by the customer but which are likely to be advantageous to him, with supporting sales argument
- advising on suitable additional quantities where a line may be underordered

- advising sales staff on which lines to push in order to maximise profitability rather than income
- establishing order priorities on a business advantage basis
- service level monitoring to improve customer perception of service quality
- research and investigation subsystems preparing current information for use by all the above
- as a possible sales aid.

9 Stock Control and Warehousing

This topic is discussed under two headings, 'Stock replacement' and 'Warehouse loading and retrieval', these being the areas within stock control and warehousing where expert system technology can make the most significant impact.

Stock replacement

The two conventional methods most often used to gauge the quantity of stock to reorder and to decide when to reorder are:

- When stock quantities fall below a certain level – the reorder threshold – sufficient stock is ordered to bring the level of stock back to a pre-specified 'ideal'. This ideal is a compromise between holding too much and tying up capital in standing stock or holding too little and running out or having to reorder frequently.
- The production plan is used to derive a material-use plan, and sufficient stock is ordered on a schedule which ensures that the production process is neither delayed nor halted temporarily because a necessary item is out of stock.

Both these methods assume that the delivery periods for reordered stock are known and stable and also that any other influencing factors (i.e. the quantity used during a reorder period) are also stable. Neither is satisfactory when conditions are volatile. There is need for a system which will not only cope with but in certain circumstances will anticipate fluctuations in its knowledge of the influencing factors. The following sections discuss ways in which expert system technology can be used within such a system to overcome the problems of instability.

Monitoring stock consumption

If the rate of stock consumption were non-variable, the reorder thresholds and reorder quantities could be fixed once and for all at suitable values. Unfortunately, the ideal of steady usage very rarely happens.

Typically, consumption of an item will vary from day to day or from week to week, but it will follow an underlying pattern, be it a weekly, monthly or yearly cycle. As an exaggerated example, an item may be consumed quickly during the first two weeks of July but very slowly during the middle weeks of September.

It is possible to monitor the continuous rates of stock withdrawal and to identify and predict patterns of consumption. Thus the reorder thresholds and quantities can be adjusted accordingly.

It is also sometimes the case that a change in the consumption of one item will influence the future consumption of another item; for example, torches and batteries or chrome articles and chrome cleaner. Using the same technology, these 'cross product' patterns can be monitored to adjust reorder thresholds and quantities as necessary.

If there is a shortage of an item and it becomes difficult or expensive to reorder, business and therefore profit will suffer. Thus it is desirable to foresee market shortages and to stockpile when necessary. In the same way, but to a lesser extent, operational costs would be

Stock Control and Warehousing

reduced if a market surplus in an item could be foreseen and stock run down to permit advantage to be taken of the likely fall in its cost. By monitoring the price of items as they are ordered and also the supplier's ability to fulfil these orders, it is possible to predict such market fluctuations and to adjust threshold (up for a potential shortage) and quantity values (up for shortage, down for surplus stock) accordingly.

Monitoring delivery periods

Typically, the time period between placing an order and taking delivery will vary from supplier to supplier. It will also vary for a particular supplier as external factors influence it; for example, during a bank holiday period or a time of high demand, the period will be longer than when the supplier is lightly loaded.

Delivery periods can be monitored using expert system technology, and the threshold for an item raised if its average delivery period is long, and lowered if it is short. It can also be adjusted when the monitoring system recognises a trend it has seen before and anticipates a lengthening in delivery period, thus reducing the danger of running out of an item during this period.

Selecting suppliers

Orders are usually placed with the supplier whose prices are the lowest available, but if price is not the priority, then we need an alternative method by which to select a supplier.

It is possible to calculate the probability of running out of an item during its delivery period, and by multiplying this by the cost to business of this happening, it is possible to obtain a valuation of an alternative supplier who will supply at a higher price but in a shorter time. The factors which determine why one supplier is used over another will change over time and by monitoring delivery times, price, order fulfilment and so on, the system can suggest changing supplier preference when appropriate.

It may be the case that one supplier has always been used because he can cope with the large orders required for item A while a second supplier is cheaper but only deals with small orders (or *vice versa*). The monitoring system may recognise a drop in the reordering frequency of item A and suggest that the second supplier is used instead of the first.

It could also suggest changing from item A to item B because it has recognised that item A's cost is increasing (or availability decreasing, etc.) and that in the past A and B have been used interchangeably.

Summary

In the foregoing, small embedded expert systems were discussed which would do the following:

- adjust re-order thresholds and reorder quantity:
    - as (or before) stock consumption fluctuates
    - to allow for suppliers having independent and fluctuating delivery periods
    - as (or before) a shortage or a surplus of an item in the market place occurs.
- Change supplier preference:
    - when the cost of a possible run-out due to a long delivery period is too high
    - when the reasons for the initial preference have changed
    - when it is both possible and preferable to substitute one item for another, where both have different suppliers.

Warehouse loading and retrieval

Usually, when stock is delivered to a store, its positioning is determined in one of two ways:
- By a system which considers predetermined parameters such as the size and weight of the items and the frequency of use (a preset value for each item).
- By a human who will consider additional factors like recent changes in the frequency of an item's use. He will always aim to store items so that his job is as straightforward as possible; items to be sent out in the near future should be on hand while those to be kept in store for a longer period may be less accessible.

There are many factors which influence this, factors which even the most experienced warehouseman cannot be expected to consider every time. In the following sections we will discuss the use of expert system technology to provide a system which will take into account some of these factors, thus making the retrieval and management of warehouse stock items more straightforward.

Positioning stock

Ideally, when a consignment of items is delivered to a warehouse, they should be placed in such a way that the next items to leave are easily accessible. At the time of storing an item, we do not always know when it will be needed next or the subequent frequency of its use, so this optimal placement is not always possible. It is possible, however, using expert system techniques to monitor the frequency of use of individual items and predict patterns of future use so that optimal positioning is achieved. For example, if a pattern suggests heavy usage for the next week followed by nothing for two weeks, then sufficient items for one week's usage can be placed readily to hand while the rest can be less accessible. Also, old stock can be moved forward (before new stock) in anticipation of use, thus aiding stock rotation.

Correlation analysis on the contents of picking lists can determine the probability that groups of items will be needed together. Clearly items which are likely to be required together should be stored together to reduce picking time. This is difficult to arrange when some items occur in many groups. A man with sufficient time could work out which items should be stored in more than one place and where they should be, but it would take a long time and would need constant revision as demand varied.

An expert system in charge of store loading can reduce picking time and cost. It can also reduce waste by correct positioning of fragile items and can arrange that old stock be used before new stock.

Planning the 'item collection' route

When an order requires many different items to be collected from around the warehouse, the collector can, by varying the collection sequence, make his job as easy or difficult as possible. Ideally he wants to walk down each aisle once, at the most, and in a sensible order (i.e. the first followed by the second etc.).

There is a much researched, much documented method within expert systems for optimal journal planning which solves what is known as 'the travelling salesman problem', this being equivalent to the problem just mentioned. By incorporating this method into a system, the best possible route will be planned for each order or collection of orders that need fulfilling.

Stock Control and Warehousing

Summary

In the foregoing the possible uses of small embedded expert systems were described:

- Planning stock-storage locations based on:
    - frequency and patterns of use – most used, most accessible and so on
    - the relationship between items when making up orders – items being stored near each other if they are frequently used within the same orders.
- Planning the optimal route by which order-making items are collected from the stores.

10 Credit Control

Credit is acquired in two ways from different sources:

- incidental to the procurement of goods and services
- as a commodity in its own right from a financial institution.

There are significant differences in the business objectives of these two classes of credit supplier which determine the control which is appropriate. Where credit is provided as an incidental, necessary to the achievement of sales of some other item, the credit cannot usually be charged for at an economic rate. Often there is no direct charge until the credit has been provided for several weeks or even months, the cost of providing credit being included in the unit cost of the item or service supplied. Thus suppliers of incidental credit wish to keep the total outstanding value as small as is consistent with other objectives. However, where credit is supplied as a commodity, it is provided at an economic rate and is, or is intended to be, profitable. Finance houses therefore wish to supply the maximum amount of credit consistent with other constraints.

Both sources share a need to limit the credit provided to a client to that which he can and will repay. There are therefore three different aspects to credit control, namely:

- establishing credit limits
- recovery of debts

Credit Control 103

- increasing sales of credit (when credit is a commodity in its own right).

Only the first two of the above aspects are discussed in this chapter. The sale of credit is an important banking activity and is discussed in the chapter on retail banking.

Establishing credit limits: suppliers of goods and services

Whenever a credit customer places an order, and every time at which goods and services are supplied to him, a decision is made as to whether or not to extend credit. That decision is usually made either by default or by comparing his total credit, assuming those goods and services are supplied within the predefined credit limit which he has been allocated.

Credit limits, when used, are set when the first effective contact with the customer is made. They may be revised at intervals and when exceptionally large orders are placed. Only rarely is there any attempt to do more than this, since credit review involves weighing up a variety of facts, uncertain information and expectations and reaching a balanced decision.

Conventionally the initial credit limit is established for business customers through the use of organisations which specialise in providing credit information, through the use of trade references, by examining published accounts and from evaluating available knowledge of that business and its managers. When the customer is an individual, a 'points' scheme is common in which a number of factors such as whether or not the prospect is a house owner, the length of time he has lived at his present address, his salary, bank references and credit card references are used to award points. His total points score is used to determine whether credit will be extended and to determine its extent.

When a business supplies customers who are individuals rather than other businesses, the number of customers is often large, since each will place relatively low-valued orders and therefore many are needed to get a satisfactory turnover. The initial credit limit is often set by a conventional system which uses correlation studies to determine the relationships between the risk of a bad debt and factors such as those listed above as relevant to point-score determination. Most points systems are crude models of the known relationships and exclude clients with good potential in the attempt to reduce bad debts. For example, the authors were involved in examining one such system which would have categorised all a particular bank's overseas vice-presidents as credit risks because they frequently moved from country to country, they rented their houses and many had no obvious ties. Clearly these people were much better credit risks than many of those whom the system would accept. Though it is not economic to build in exception conditions specifically for bank vice-presidents, there are many other similar exceptions which it is difficult to build into a conventional system. A very small rule-based module can be much more selective, both as to those who are accepted and those who are rejected, so widening the potential client base and reducing the number of bad debts. A typical point-evaluation system can be converted into about twenty rules. Another twenty or thirty can make a considerable difference to profit by increasing the number of good-risk clients which are accepted and also the number of bad risks which are rejected. This application is both fast and simple to implement and often profitable.

The prediction of business failure, an important part of the credit decision for corporate clients, is a particularly difficult area. The problem has, of course, been studied extensively, but there is no clear safe guidance available. One possible AI solution involves the use of arithmetic selection, ratios, and so on, to reject the obviously

Credit Control

unsuitable and then an 'expert accountant' system which classifies the remainder into groups on the basis of its assessment of the degree of risk. A human accountant examines the contents of each group and identifies any items which he considers to be wrongly classified. Then he feeds back to the system his reasons for disagreeing and so extends the rule base. This is an example of a learning system where the system improves with time. Its initial benefits are solely those of enabling the human accountant to give priority to the best applicants but, as it learns, it will eventually be capable of the complete task.

There are hidden difficulties with this application which are worth examining. One of the problems is that of obtaining the necessary information on the target companies. The rules added by the accountant may relate to items of information which do not appear in the accounts themselves; for example, they often refer to information in the Annual Report and can only be found by reading through the text. As the system grows there may eventually be many such items of information, each occurring very infrequently, thus creating a difficult search problem for any novice who may consult the system in the future. Moreover, there is a further difficulty in recognising that two differently expressed statements are conceptually identical unless the user has a thorough grounding in the subject. Often the conceptual information is implicit rather than explicit and both intelligence and knowledge are required to extract that information and so determine that it is relevant input to the expert system. The human expert, in this case the accountant, hardly notices this difficulty and may be able to increase the knowledge of the system to the point where it can give the same answers as he does – so long as he or some other expert is preparing the information for it; the system may still be of little value if fed by a novice.

The authors believe that systems such as this will in

time become very valuable but that the problems associated with providing the input will be difficult to handle until the problem of natural language understanding has been solved. One might find that a trained but experienced junior accountant could work with such a system but that even so it is not likely to be a cost-effective opportunity for the use of AI by the ordinary supplier of goods and services.

This example is interesting in that it illustrates one of the problems in identifying suitable AI opportunities, namely that of understanding where and how knowledge and intelligence are applied to solve a problem. It is easy to miss some important task which, though essential, does not appear to be part of the problem being studied.

Establishing credit limits: financial institutions

As we have just seen, suppliers of goods and services on credit are mainly concerned with establishing the credit worthiness of prospective clients up to the value of the goods and services sold. Financial institutions, however, provide credit as a principle business activity and so wish to provide each client with the maximum safe amount. There are exceptions, such as hire purchase finance, where there is a natural limit in the value of goods, but even in this case the finance house may wish to offer other credit to suitable clients. Thus a significant difference between the two funding sources is that suppliers work to a natural cut-off and institutions to the maximum safe limit. One could regard suppliers as binary in that either a customer can have credit or he cannot; whereas institutions could be regarded as having a sliding scale in that a customer can have x amount of credit where x is the safe limit associated with him. The second difference is that as credit supply is such an important business activity of institutions, it must be profitable for them.

These differences do not change the nature of the credit assessment process, but they do change the amount of effort which may be expended economically to improve the quality of the credit limit decision. Thus the number of factors considered in the 'points' score, the value of improving its accuracy and the likely benefits of replacing a purely numeric score method by a knowledge-base design are all greater. The accountant expert system is more likely to be of value here also; since the number of credit decisions is likely to be higher, there is increased value in getting each correct and the institutions are more likely to have junior staff who are financially trained and so capable of interpreting input for it.

Ongoing credit decisions

When an existing credit customer wishes to reorder or a financial institution's client wishes to extend or to renew a facility, there is an opportunity to revise the credit decision and also new information on which this decision may be based.

These credit decisions can utilise updated financial information. They can also draw on the past history of the client's payments and on his previous business volumes, thus allowing the estimates of risk and profit to be improved. The methods described above can be used for credit revision if provision is made for the inclusion of new information and if appropriate changes are made to the implications attached to some of the conditions in the initial credit-setting function. For example, the initial credit-setting function may contain a rule which prohibits credit being given to someone who has just moved house, but we would not want to refuse credit to a customer who we have traded with for many years simply because he moves house.

Minimising credit

To reduce the quantity of credit supplied, one needs alternative methods of payment which secure earlier payment for goods purchased. Earlier payment is secured by several devices which include:
- payment with order
- down payment with order
- cash on delivery
- stage payments
- hire purchase funding
- early settlement discounts
- punitive interest charges on late payments
- debt chasing.

Even if one did not know the critical importance of this aspect of credit control to cash flow and corporate health, one might infer it from the number of methods generally used to restrict or monitor the amount of credit taken.

Obviously the 'standard terms of trade' have to be adjusted according to circumstances. They define the terms considered appropriate to the average customer. Their use permits the duplication of forms, avoids the need to make decisions on every individual case and facilitates control over the legal position. An expert system which monitors payment history and business volume would enable individual decisions to be made more easily. It could arrange for special forms to be produced containing the right terms for each customer, and it could ensure that all terms offered were in accordance with policy. For example, it might recommend that one customer should only be supplied against

Credit Control

an initial payment whilst another should be supplied against payment via hire purchase. The expertise required to recommend alternative terms of payment for individual customers must be sufficient to:

- classify them into groups reflecting the profit expected from their future business
- estimate the cost of credit associated with each of the possible methods of credit containment
- estimate the cost of lost business which is associated with each method.

The basic rules are fairly simple, but there are often a lot of special cases which increase the number of rules. This is why a 'recommending' rather than a 'deciding' system is suggested, allowing the human to handle the unusual exceptions. This possible application has much in common with that discussed earlier in Chapter 8 'Sales and Order Entry', which was also concerned with the strategic importance of customers to future profit. It can be a part of the same process of account management, and if both applications are implemented, they can share information, some of the processing and their conclusions.

Summary

Three possible embedded AI applications have been discussed in this chapter. The first two are credit-rating applications, one being a very small knowledge-based subsystem and the other a large and difficult one from which the return is dependent on the circumstances in which it is used. They are:

a point-score replacement
an 'expert accountant'.

The inclusion of either in the credit-rating system would assist both the initial and any later credit risk assessments.

The third application is a 'terms of trade' advisor.

11 Management Information

Managers are heavy users of information. They need an overview of everything that happens in their field of accountability. They must also be able to find out details on any matter of concern or interest. Moreover, a manager uses information for a wide range of purposes, each requiring the information available to be combined and presented differently.

The volume of data which passes through a business, even the simplest business, is large. Each individual item of data, taken alone, is practically meaningless. One problem faced by every manager is that of managing data, of having it converted from its elemental form into some other in which its meaning may be readily understood so that the business can be effectively controlled. What is more, the solution to that problem must minimise the costs of collecting, storing and processing information.

Managers use information:

- as a means of measuring the degree to which actual achievement meets expectations
- to determine whether their objectives are likely to be attained
- to estimate the probable outcome of possible decisions and actions
- to schedule activities and resources
- to prepare reports for the managers above them in the hierarchy

- to prepare reports for others such as central government.

The correct use of information is an essential part of the manager's task.

Management information systems must fulfil a variety of needs. In particular they must achieve the following goals:

- provide means of determining whether the business is on course, particularly in critical areas
- identify any areas in which the business is off course, including both those areas where results are worse and also those which are better than expected
- facilitate investigation and detailed examination of any area, particularly but not exclusively those areas where the results are exceptional
- assist in the preparation of forecasts
- assist in the selection of plans which will achieve the business objectives
- prepare statutory reports and other standard reports.

Conventional management information systems

The conventional management information system incorporates an extensive data base and provides information in two forms. The first of these is a standard summary in a predefined format which is produced at regular intervals. It is supplied to managers to provide the overview they need and to answer common questions of detail. It can also be used to identify any exceptional areas which warrant action or further investigation. Most businesses use a variety of these information summaries, some being summaries of key factors for individual parts of the business, others being summaries of the whole business which are derived from a single

Management Information

computer or manual system. One variant of this is the 'exception report' which was developed to reduce the volume of information presented to a manager. This report uses a standard format but excludes items where the 'actuals' are within a permitted variance of the 'budgets' for those items.

The second means of presenting information allows further investigation into detail unavailable from the overall summary. The systems which do this vary greatly in capability. The system may be very simple, allowing only for the printing of detailed lists which must be examined at the elementary level. It may provide selective printing facilities, include provisions for the production and run of special-purpose enquiry programs, or even allow the manager to specify directly to the machine what he wants presented to him.

Conventional management information systems vary widely in capability and complexity, but in general they are:

- containers of very important corporate assets
- an imperfect means of identifying problem areas
- difficult to focus on a specific problem
- often difficult for a manager to use effectively
- overproductive of detail and paper.

AI technology in information systems

Management is a highly skilled operation. Even the selection of information for management use requires a high level of expertise. AI technology has a long way to go before an artificial 'expert manager' can be built and even a 'management information selector' is impractical. There are, however, a number of tasks where AI technology may make a contribution. These include the following, which are discussed below:

- expert interfaces for management use
- assistance in the preparation of strategic overviews
- the identification of points which need special attention.

Expert interfaces

Systems with extensive capabilities are hard to use. Training helps, but where there are many capabilities, each of which is seldom required, the details of how to use them are soon forgotten. Careful systems design can make them simpler to use, and help facilities can ease the problem, but neither provides a complete solution. This is a field where an expert interface can be particularly useful. These interfaces assist inexperienced or untrained users to obtain the information which they want from their data base by allowing them to key in their query in English rather than a complicated data-base language or code. Microdata's 'English' is an intelligent language system of this type.

Systems such as this allow the enquirer to ask questions without knowing where the data he needs is stored, how to access it or even what its name is. They can combine the content of a series of questions, preserving knowledge of the question context. For example, if the question 'How many customers live in London?' was followed by 'How many buy product X?', the second question would be interpreted as meaning 'How many of the customers who live in London buy product X?' If the next question were 'And in Tokyo?' the system would ask for further explanation as in this case the context does not make it clear whether the question refers to all customers in Tokyo or only those who buy product X.

When such a system is to be used directly by managers they may be dissuaded from using it by the need to key in their requirements, since very few managers are also competent keyboard operators. A word or continuous-speech interpreting subsystem can simplify this problem. A true 'speech understanding' system is not needed. The purpose of the subsystem is only to replace the use of the keyboard and it need only recognise words which are in the enquiry system dictionary.

Identification of exceptions

Exception reporting is the identification of those areas where the actual performance differs significantly from that which was forecast. It is intended to direct management attention at those points where something is going wrong, with a view to correcting it, and also to those points where something is going unexpectedly well, where there may be a possibility of exploiting an advantage. The approach is attractive but the method is not used extensively for several reasons, in particular the following:

- Certain exceptional items are not controllable or do not require management attention. For example, expenditure may exceed forecast as a result of a non-recurring purchase following a management decision made in response to an unexpected and therefore unplanned event. Thus a special offer of some item can result in a management decision to purchase additional stock and so increase the stock-holding cost. Further management action is necessary, even though the holding cost is higher than was planned. As a second example, a business may loose a dispute and have to pay damages and legal fees. No management action can avoid that payment or future repetitions.
- The serious exceptions may lie in the simultaneous occurrence of a number of small variations rather

than in any one. If these variations fall within the tolerance level of the system, then they will be identified and the cumulative effect passes unnoticed. If the tolerance level is lowered to prevent this, then a large number of irrelevant variations will be reported as exceptional. The minimum level to avoid the swamping effect is often higher than the maximum level needed to detect small cumulatively important variations.
- When an exception has been identified, management needs additional detailed information to decide on the action to take. If the system presents only the global exception, then there is a delay whilst the detailed information is obtained.

The problem of including within management information details of exceptional events which are outside, or do not require, management control cannot be avoided without risking the exclusion of some exceptions of a similar nature which do require management control. If the system is efficient in drawing attention to those exceptional events which it is intended to highlight, then the problem of occasionally having other events unnecessarily highlighted is small compared to the benefits which the system can provide.

The second problem, of identifying only those small variations which are significant and not the vast majority which are of no concern, is similar to the above problem. It is again a trade-off between being provided with too much information or too little. It is a compromise, and where the tolerance level is positioned will depend on the preference of the manager or managers concerned.

Once an exception condition has been detected through the use of summary information, the manager will wish to obtain more detailed information on the problem. The details required will include those which were incorporated into the summary, but often information is needed from other related areas. Assimilated detail is used to pinpoint the cause; detail from elsewhere is required where the action may be to offset the first variation by another. An expert subsystem can be used to backtrack through a conventional system finding the detail items which made up the exceptional total and to determine which of those details vary from the norm to contribute to the exception originally identified. Sometimes the cause will be specific individual items, sometimes it will be the coincidence of a number of normal but occasional items.

This leads to a possible means of segregating the influence of large exceptional individual items from the accumulated overview. Two sets of figures can be provided, one including and the other excluding the exceptional items which can be listed and evaluated separately. Those items on this separate list which require no action can then be ignored. The report which excludes all exceptional items is used to reveal the small simultaneous exceptions for which action may be necessary.

There is scope for a number of different levels of expert assistance here which simplify the task of directing attention to the most useful areas.

Investigations

Investigations into particular circumstances or into the reasons for the values of totals can usually be performed effectively by means of a good conventional data-base system. The principle exception where AI techniques can be useful is for those enquiries where imprecise questioning is necessary. For example, one might want a list of staff who are about twenty-five years old, earn about £12,000 per annum and live near Manchester. Fuzzy search methods carry out searches of this kind, ordering the results so that those who are 'direct hits' – that is, those who are exactly twenty-five, earn exactly £12,000 per annum and who live in Manchester – are presented first with those who 'nearly fit' presented next. They are often used in AI and are accepted AI techniques.

Standard reports

Standard predefined reports do not normally benefit from the inclusion of AI techniques, but there are a few situations where it is convenient to define a few rules which are applied to the data to vary the application of standard formats. For example, there may be combinations of circumstances in which a detailed breakdown is desirable and others in which it is not. AI rules which enable the system to differentiate between such cases and alter the format accordingly would be useful.

Summary

AI techniques may be useful for the following purposes in a management information system:

- to give expert interfaces for special enquiries
- to allow speech input to the interface
- to identify exceptions
- to breakdown exception areas to detail
- to identify and isolate exceptional individual items
- for multiple 'fuzzy' enquiries.

12 Business Planning

Planning includes the following tasks:

- forecasting the future environment; for example, market size, competition, resource availability
- forecasting the values of critical factors of the business in that environment; for example, sales volume by product
- forecasting resources
- considering what alternative actions there may be
- forecasting the results of taking actions, alone or in combination
- selecting a set of actions which are likely to result in a satisfactory outcome.

The possible application of AI in business planning is discussed below under these six subject areas.

All the possible applications are for expert systems, principally for expert assistants. The authors have found business planning to be somewhat disappointing in that fewer possibilities have been found than one would expect, and most of those are only likely to be economic under special circumstances.

The future environment

Forecasts of the future are derived from many sources, one of which is the records of the business. Expert systems may be of use in identifying underlying general trends, cyclic patterns, and so on, which are obscured by random variations, and the authors and their colleagues have installed a system in one business which is used for this purpose.

However, some of the sources from which future forecasts can be delivered are not amenable to such examination. For example, some may be direct forecasts bought in a ready-processed form from a market survey company without the detailed history that such a system would require. In this instance, any expert system would be used by the market survey company, not by its clients.

Critical business factors

Forecasting critical business factors such as sales by product line in the future environment normally draws heavily on previous corporate experience. Conventional methods of forecasting are usually adequate given the uncertainty level of all the values used, but there are situations where an expert system can be a worthwhile addition. For example, when there are a number of factors which are known to influence the sales of a product but they are not known well enough for the mathematical relationship to be expressed as an algorithm, a small expert system which stores the rules as they are perceived to be can be useful. In this instance a stand-alone system or shell in which an AI language is used (in much the same way as a spread-sheet package) is the typical implementation means.

Ideally the forecaster should use the language directly, adjusting the rules himself as he works. It is seldom practical to use a professional programmer to make the changes for the same reasons that spread-sheet formulae are better entered by their users. AI languages require more training than spread-sheets, but it is practical to train an intelligent man who is not a skilled programmer

Business Planning

to adapt an existing program and a few days of training should suffice for this purpose.

The use of an expert system in this role has three benefits. First, the system may actually save time and effort. Second, it ensures that when an estimate or forecast is made, none of the rules are forgotten. Third, the knowledge of which things to consider when making a forecast, and other relevant knowledge, is often limited to a few experienced staff. When this knowledge is only available through the use of specific individuals there is risk of its loss. When the knowledge is stored in a system it becomes a corporate asset.

Resource requirements

Conventional software, spread-sheet software in particular, is normally quite adequate for resource planning. An expert assistant can be useful when there are alternative means of providing the necessary resources, such as when a single resource can be used in one or other of two ways or when schedules can be varied. Such instances can occur when it is desired to plan the resource use in detail and the resources are manufacturing tools with multiple capabilities or are staff who each have several relevant skills. A rule-based system can then be used to find an effective work allocation or to reveal any discrepancy between the resources needed and those available.

To illustrate this point, consider the following very small example. Assume that there are two employees who include amongst their skills plumbing, bricklaying and carpentry. The work calls for a plumber and a bricklayer. It is only possible to do both simultaneously if the carpenter is also a plumber or a bricklayer. It is not feasible if both the skills which are needed are only available in the same individual.

Scheduling when there are a number of individuals each with different combinations of skills can become very difficult to perform by hand or by conventional systems. Linear programming can be used, but it solves the problem for one moment in time, not against a schedule.

Identifying possible actions

Determining what possible actions could be taken to improve the results of a business is a highly skilled task. Some of those possibilities will need expertise specific to the particular business; for example, knowledge of its productive capability or of the needs of its customers. Other possibilities will require less specific expertise, knowledge applicable to a particular industry or even knowledge which is general to most businesses, such as expertise in selecting correctly from the alternative methods of funding a business.

Building an expert system to store the expertise required to identify business-specific alternative actions is generally an uneconomic proposition. It is a large and expensive task which takes too long. It can, however, be practical where the business is repetitive and very closely focused, as is the case with franchise operations, for example.

Where the expertise is less specific and so can be applied to a number of businesses which have similar problems and similar possible solutions, the development of an expert system to suggest possible actions can be both feasible and cost-effective. This implies that the costs will be spread by making it available as a service. The service will be limited, however, since expertise which is business-specific cannot of course be incorporated. A bank might provide the use of an intelligent system to help its customers identify funding options, or

Business Planning

an agricultural advisory service might offer farmers the use of a system to identify suitable farming options.

Summary

The AI techniques which have been discussed above include:

- identification of patterns and trends
- forecasting when relationships are imprecisely known
- scheduling multi-purpose resources
- advising on corrective actions.

13 Production Scheduling

The primary objective of production scheduling is to use production resources in the best possible way. The word 'best' implies a balanced achievement of subsidiary objectives which are frequently incompatible. They include:
- Ensuring the satisfaction of customers. This may mean attempting equally to fill all orders by due dates, or it may mean giving priority to certain customers because of their strategic importance or to certain orders which are urgently required or which have penalty clauses attached. It may mean ensuring that stock levels are maintained on a full range of different products. Often it means simultaneously achieving all the above and more.
- Maximising the efficiency of use of scarce resources to maximise income. For example, if a particular raw material which is used in varying amounts in a number of products is scarce, it may be best to schedule those products which are the lowest users of that material first. Then, if the next delivery is delayed, the existing stock will last longer and production can continue. The schedule should also take account of the profit margin associated with each alternative use of the scarce resource and should aim to ensure that the most profitable uses have priority. The scarce resource may not, of course, necessarily be a raw material. It may be plant

storage space, particular skills or any other possible constraint on production.
- Minimising production costs. This may involve maximising batch sizes to reduce the cost of unproductive set-up times. It may mean combining jobs to minimise material waste. It may mean reducing the work load on specific high-cost plant. For instance, older tools which are worn may produce an above-average reject rate or they may be slow in operation and so have a higher operator cost.
- Providing for necessary 'non-productive' activities such as safety and maintenance inspections, plant overhauls, the installation of new equipment, staff training and so on.

Scheduling systems

Conventional production scheduling systems do not and cannot allow for all the subsidiary objectives listed above. They are often restricted to producing a feasible work programme which will use available plant and labour to meet defined quantity objectives for stated products. A priority system for particular orders is a frequent addition.

This is clearly a field where the use of AI can benefit a business. The nature of the problem, to achieve a suitable balance between a number of sub-objectives using information that is often uncertain, is a typical indicator of an expert system opportunity. The difficulty lies in the size of the expert system that would be needed if one were to attempt a total solution.

To obtain benefits within a reasonably short time it is necessary to be selective. For example, one might build a hybrid system in which parts of the work were done by small intelligent systems which passed their results to a conventional production scheduler. The scheduler could in turn be used as a tool by an intelligent program which would supply it with different instructions on each cycle and so, by trial, error and intelligent choice of instructions, work towards an optimal solution. This approach is crude and inelegant, but it can be developed in a relatively short time and can be used to concentrate work on those areas where the need and the potential benefits are greatest.

The following paragraphs suggest a few of the subsidiary problems which might justify an intelligent solution.

Multiple capability resource scheduling

Scheduling becomes more difficult when resources have multiple capabilities in different combinations; for example, where employees each have several skills. This problem has already been discussed in the previous chapter as a business-planning problem, but it and the suggested approach are equally applicable to production scheduling.

Batch and run-sizing

In many industries where products are made against estimated demand, particular products are made in batches to share set-up costs over a number of units. There may also be groups of similar products such that the time required to change set-up from one product to another in the group is less than to change to a completely different product. Unit costs of production can be minimised by increasing batch sizes and by sequencing products such that the overall set-up time is minimised. However, as batch sizes are increased, the number of units stocked is also increased, thus adding to the cost of storage.

Using conventional calculation methods, batch sizes

are established on the basis of set-up costs, item value and storage space costs. But these are all notional costs. If the raw materials and plant are available, the actual cost of increasing a batch size is the loss of an opportunity to use that raw material for some other purpose. True storage costs depend on the actual storage space available and the cost of not using that space for something else. If it is available and there is no other use for it, the cost of using it is zero. A better return can be obtained from the investment made by deciding on batch sizes individually and in the light of prevailing conditions. However, those decisions require some intelligence and expertise.

Service level monitoring

Chapter 8 mentions the use of service level monitoring as a sales aid. Briefly, it involves a continuous watch on the overall level of service provided to customers, particularly to key customers, to ensure that the cumulative effect of the service to those customers is identified. As stated in Chapter 8, that monitoring should span the complete operation from sales through to post-delivery attention for maximum effectiveness.

Service level monitoring in production scheduling is practical as a separate entity even when not part of a complete monitoring system. For each order, records are maintained of customer, required delivery date, scheduled date and actual delivery date. The implications of this historical data are inferred by an expert system. An assessment of the overall service level is provided and warning is given if it is deduced that the customer is likely to be dissatisfied. These warnings can be used to raise the scheduling priority of that customer's current orders.

Rescheduling following divergence from plan

The application described below is particularly relevant to tightly scheduled operations such as those of a flexible manufacturing system call.

The initial schedule is established using standard times for each operation. As work proceeds and stages are completed, there may be variations between actual and standard times. Those variations in time will have causes which may be deduced from an examination of those variations. For example, on a drilling platform, a reduced oil pressure may result in swarf being cleared slowly and in reduced cutting speeds irrespective of the tool, whereas a blunt tool will only cause delays until the defective tool is replaced.

If the causes of variations from the established schedule are known, a new schedule can be prepared which makes allowance for them, either by allowing for their correction or for their continuance. The fault diagnosis required for this purpose involves categorising faults. Since the faults within any one category have similar results, there is no need for a complete fault analyser. The expert system required is thus a relatively simple one.

Summary

Production scheduling operations can be improved by the inclusion of expert systems to achieve a wide variety of objectives. The following examples have been discussed:

- overall optimisation of resource use in conjunction with a standard scheduling system
- true cost batch and run sizing
- service level monitoring and order priority setting
- multiple capability resource scheduling
- rescheduling to allow for possible faults or delays.

14 Preventive Maintenance

When a piece of machinery fails, the costs incurred often include, not just those of replacement or repair, but additional costs consequent upon the failure of the item whilst it is in service. If a car breaks down, its driver and passengers may lose valuable time and perhaps have to pay hotel bills. If a water-pump breaks down in use, then extensive damage may be done by flooding.

It is sometimes possible to reduce the frequency of 'on the job' failures by taking action to forestall them. There are two ways in which this may be done. One way is to predict when a failure is likely and arrange to stop the use of the item prior to the predicted time of failure (failure prediction). The other is to take action to increase the period between failures (preventive maintenance). Failure prediction and preventive maintenance are closely related. Failure prediction is sometimes carried out whilst a machine is in operation. By monitoring its vibration signal, impending failures can be predicted and the machine can be halted at a convenient point prior to failure. AI systems can be used for this task, but this is not preventive maintenance and so no discussion of these 'real time' systems is included in this chapter.

This chapter is concerned with the establishment of predefined work undertaken at predefined intervals, such as the replacement of a car's engine oil to increase the engine life or the replacement of aircraft parts after a specified number of flying hours. There are two reasons for preventive maintenance:

- to decrease the possibility of actual failure
- to reduce an efficiency loss which would otherwise occur (e.g. one may replace an air filter on a vacuum cleaner in order to maintain an effective vacuum pressure and so minimise the time taken to clean a floor).

The costs and benefits of preventive maintenance

A full evaluation of the costs and benefits of preventive maintenance involves:
- estimating the probabilities of failure from different causes both if the maintenance is done and if it is not done
- estimating differences in efficiency with or without maintenance
- estimating repair and maintenance costs
- valuing the consequential costs of an in-service breakdown (these usually depend on when the breakdown occurs so this involves estimating the probability of a breakdown under each relevant different condition).

These estimates are then used in a long and complex equation to calculate the benefit (positive or negative) of carrying out the maintenance tasks under consideration at the particular time concerned.

Naturally enough, no one attempts to estimate all the various probabilities which should be considered. Instead, a few of the key costs are estimated and the probabilities are simplified by grouping them. Then, if there are enough breakdowns to analyse and obtain meaningful results, the failure rates with and without the proposed maintenance are measured.

These simplifications provide a workable method, but this does have a number of quite serious disadvantages.

Preventive Maintenance

First, as we do not have a full mathematical model, we cannot explore the possibilities of different combinations of maintenance activities. Instead, we rely on individual component failure to indicate what activities should be performed together. This gives us no means of detecting over-engineered and uneconomic maintenance, and no effective means of determining economic maintenance intervals. Second, all occurrences of the same class of item are treated as being identical. In practice two apparently identical items of plant are neither identical nor do they experience identical conditions of use. The economic maintenance level for an item is actually specific to that item, though it does have similarities which are appropriate to other members of its class. The result is that preventive maintenance is not as cost-effective as it might be; we pay more and get less benefit. To improve the position, we need better information on faults and their costs, and we need a more effective means of planning preventive maintenance.

Reducing cost and improving quality

In addition to working out more accurately what preventive maintenance should be done and when, one may also be able to reduce the cost of doing it. The quality of the maintenance might also be improved to obtain a larger reduction in the failure rate. These points are closely linked and are aspects of working methods.

The cost and the quality of work are both largely determined by the degree to which the maintenance engineer knows what he should do, how he should best do it and by his having the correct tools and materials with him. This is obviously desirable but difficult to achieve. It is even more difficult if the maintenance required by an individual item of plant is specific to that item.

Opportunities for the use of AI

The examples selected from this field of work and outlined very briefly in the following subsections are:

- failure analysis
- maintenance planning
- maintenance kit preparation
- *idiot savant* maintenance aid.

Other possible areas to look at which are not discussed further include:

- post-repair test assistant
- maintenance scheduling
- maintenance variation following an on-the-job failure
- in-maintenance variations and kit supply
- analysis of repair kit items returned to store to deduce the extra work done during maintenance visits.

Failure analysis

Failure analysis can be used to derive failure rates by:

- part
- the conditions prevalent at the time of failure
- the cost of the failure
- the cost of repair/replacement
- what other work was done on the item during the repair (e.g. suppose that in repairing an item the existing gaskets which did not fail are replaced; the gasket failure rate, and the need to replace gaskets, will now be that of new gaskets rather than that of old ones).

Failure information is often difficult to obtain as a direct input since breakdown engineers either do not report at all or else do so incompletely. Additional information is

Preventive Maintenance

required. There are several possible sources of that information additional to the obvious reflection, in returns or orders, of store-item consumption. For example, production control systems often show delays due to plant failure and the like. The information received from each source is probably imprecise and incomplete but often, when it is combined, one can deduce what items of plant broke down and what work was done to repair them. Though a human can make these deductions, it would take too long to be cost-effective. A system which has access to these information sources can make its deductions in a cost-effective time. One way of simplifying the deductive process required and simultaneously improving the quality of the final result is to use the failure analysis system to give its conclusions to the maintenance engineer or to ask explicitly for further information where no conclusion can be reached.Though engineers usually dislike reporting, they are willing to make corrections and provide assistance if asked.

Maintenance planning

The problems faced in deciding what maintenance of an item will be most cost-effective have been discussed above. Even if an intelligent fault analyser is used to improve knowledge of those factors which are needed by the full mathematical model, it is not likely that all the factors will become known with sufficient accuracy to make that model usable as a planning tool. Moreover, even if that model were completely available, there would still be some difficulty in its use. It can only value preselected groups of maintenance activities; it cannot itself both propose and evaluate a service plan. What is needed is some means of obtaining a satisfactory solution, despite the gaps in the model, which will work out a service plan and will do so sufficiently cheaply that it can be reapplied regularly as more information becomes available, as plant ages and as the conditions in which it is used change.

An expert system which would do this well would require a large knowledge base extracted from engineers and accountants, and it would only be a cost-justifiable undertaking for the largest organisations. However, as there is so little done at present, even a simple and not very knowledgeable system may be able to make a contribution. Note that this opportunity is one which can expand beyond all hope of financial return and that if an implementation is undertaken it should be closely monitored.

Maintenance kit preparation

This is a very simple application which can be serviced by a small embedded expert system. It can make a significant reduction in costs when the maintenance is carried out on location and thus at a distance from stores. The objective is to provide the maintenance engineer with a kit which is based on his planned work for the period for which he is away from the stores; that is, usually for a day's work. The kit comprises:

- those items which he should use for the work; that is, items which are listed for mandatory replacement
- those items which he may require and where the probability of his requiring them is sufficient to justify their inclusion in the kit
- a list of jobs which he might consider necessary as a result of his inspections (not necessarily an exhaustive list) which he does not have the equipment with him to complete, showing in each case whether or not the equipment required is available in stock.

The list is included to assist him in deciding, in doubtful cases, whether or not he should commence an optional

Preventive Maintenance

repair or replacement. If the list shows that an item which is needed for a repair or replacement is not in stock, then he will decide against the extra maintenance. Also, if he has a choice of either replacing an item or repairing it, and the list shows that while the item is not in stock, the components necessary to its repair are, then he will repair rather than replace.

The benefit of the system lies in its ability to reduce the number of trips required to maintain equipment on-site when it is not feasible to carry a complete set of spares. This can be the case when maintaining equipment on a client's site under a fixed-rate maintenance contract.

The store-item picking list can be prepared by a conventional system against the maintenance engineer's work plan, lists of standard jobs and stock records. The intelligent subsystem can contribute by taking an overall view of the total requirement. This involves examining the likely need for specific parts during the day across the plan as a whole, the combinations of parts which may be needed to complete tasks, the availability of items in the stores in the combinations which may be needed and the limitations on the engineer's capability to transport items.

Idiot savant maintenance aid

This is a simplified version of a classic expert system application. The classic expert repair system can give advice on the diagnosis of faults in the equipment in which it is expert, it can advise on how to dismantle, to repair and restore the machine, and it can give explanatory information on why it makes those recommendations. Such systems can be very useful when the repairman is wholly unfamiliar with the plant, and they often fulfil a dual role of securing an effective repair and of teaching the repairman.

If the maintenance engineers have been trained, however, as is usually the case, they will not need that detailed assistance. What they may need is access to information contained in the appropriate reference manual and a few warnings as to sequence of operations or combinations of activities which can cause trouble. For example, a warning might indicate that either part A or part B can be removed without trouble, but that if both are removed simultaneously damage or additional work is likely. Such a system may also include information on previous versions of the equipment and more detail still on versions which are obsolete and seldom encountered.

The implementation is, in effect, a shortened version of the traditional repair assistant, which displays reference material to avoid the need to go into detail and only provides diagnostic advice where conditions are exceptional. The foreshortening reduces the work needed to get it operational and does not significantly reduce its value when used by trained staff.

Summary

Of the nine possible applications for AI mentioned in this chapter the following four were discussed:
- Failure analysis, which increases the information available on component failure frequencies.
- Maintenance planning, which can improve the cost-effectiveness of preventive maintenance. Careful control of this application is essential as it tends to grow beyond the optimum return point.
- Maintenance kit preparation, which can reduce site visits and is of most value when maintenance sites are distant from stores.
- Idiot savant maintenance aid – a much simplified version of a well-known expert system.

15 Manufacturing

There is widespread recognition that not only will AI be of value in production work of the future but it can be of use now, although the profitability of using it may be in doubt. There is therefore less need to identify possible opportunities in this field than in others, and this chapter is provided more to act as a reminder than to offer new thinking.

The main areas where AI can assist in the production process are:

- Design work:
    - adding design details, acting as an assistant to a designer
    - searching a design for possible faults and weaknesses
    - amending a design to reduce costs or to improve maintainability.
- Plant and tools:
    - fully automatic intelligent tools and plant
    - numerically controlled (pre-programmed) tools with intelligent overrides
    - operator-controlled tools with the ability to interpret detail intelligently.
- Operator assistance:
    - operator guidance for unskilled operatives
    - voice-controlled operation and variants.
- Transport:
    - intelligent vehicles

- intelligent recognition and switching of parts on conveyor systems.
- Tool shops:
  - tool recognition, post-use inspection and storage.

'Manufacturing' covers the production of so many different things, and so many different processes are used to produce them that there is little to be gained from any general description of purpose or for work content. It is also a fruitful field in which to search for AI opportunities to improve the quality of a product or to reduce costs and so make a significant contribution to profitability. The following examples from a variety of different manufacturing environments indicate what can be done.

The AI applications selected for discussion are:

- rapid stabilisation following a step change in the inputs of a continuous process
- speech control of an assembly-line tool
- FMS cell transport control
- flash removal from moulded plastic
- selection of part-used sheet material.

Rapid stabilisation of a continuous process

Process control theory is based on the principle that the inputs to the process comprise both controllable and uncontrollable variables and that the desired output can be restored, when an uncontrollable variable changes value, by adjusting the values of one or more of the controllable variables. The control task is complicated by the fact that often the values of some of the uncontrollable variables cannot be measured directly. If one of these changes value, then the first measurable event is a change in the quality of the output. The output does not change until it incorporates the result of the changed

Manufacturing

input, so there is a delay between the change occurring and it becoming measurable, which is equal to the process time.

Changes can be gradual, as for example when a tool wears or when temperature changes, or they may be stepped as when one batch of raw material is exhausted and the next batch of a different quality enters the system. Often the uncontrollable variables are subject to step changes whilst the controllable variables (when they have been altered to counteract changes in uncontrollable variables) can only provide gradual change. This leads to further delays whilst equilibrium is restored. The process delay combined with the time needed to correct a step change by using a gradual change can mean that product quality is below standard for a considerable period of time.

Where the input stream incorporates more than one uncontrollable variable, or where the value of such a variable is volatile, the control task can become very difficult, and the proportion of rejected output can become unacceptable. This leads to the procurement of more expensive, quality-standardised raw materials to give stability to the system.

The inclusion of an expert system in the control module may assist in reducing the time taken to restore stability, particularly where multiple-step changes, whether they be due to volatility of one variable or changes in several variables, can occur. There are two approaches which can be used singly or in combination.

First, although the values of the uncontrollable variables in the input to the system may not be directly measurable, it may be possible to obtain indicative information. The following example is simple and could be resolved in other ways, but it illustrates the point. Suppose the process to be that of blending: the uncontrollable variables are the nature of three vegetable products; the controllable variables are the proportion of each in the blend; and the measurable product-quality is taste. Deliveries of ingredients from different sources will vary and the taste of each cannot be quantified. Some general observations can be made, however; for example:

- the probability associated with each proportion of each ingredient in the product mix (e.g. the probability that ingredient 'A' should be one-third of the mix)
- the correlation between colour or moisture content (measurable) and flavour strength (non-measurable)
- the correlation between geographic source and flavour
- significant changes only occur when batches change
- quality changes from unchanged batches do not require corrective action; they are only temporary.

Rules such as these cannot define the correct mix, but they can be used to obtain a reasonable approximation of what it is likely to be and to indicate when the mix proportions are likely to need changing.

The second approach is as follows. Traditionally the controlled variable is continually adjusted depending on the remaining difference between the actual and the desired outputs. It is sometimes possible to use 'expertise' to give a close estimate of the total change in the controlled variable to close in on stability more quickly.

Referring to the previous example involving the mixing of natural vegetable products, suppose the current batch of ingredient 'A' has an unusually strong flavour. When this batch is replaced by another with the normal, weaker flavour, we can expect the new mix to need more of the weaker flavoured 'A' and make an adjustment as the new batch enters the hopper. We may even be able to do better than this and deduce the most likely combination from other physical properties.

Speech control on an assembly-line tool

In this example the operation required both hands to hold large flat sheets of material and the operator had previously to let go with one hand to operate the machine. The problem was reduced by arranging for the controlling system to infer what was required and to display that proposal. The operative then used key words to change the display as he thought appropriate and finally used one single physical control to actuate the process.

The use of a single physical control such as holding down a foot bar can thus be used to perform any function or function sequence. The combination of voice and physical switch is a convenient safety precaution where the process might be harmful if initiated by chance. A display was used because the input information needed for a process series was voluminous. Had it been simple, the operative could have been informed by voice synthesiser of the machine's suggested input. In this example, voice synthesis was used to confirm the correct receipt of key words spoken by the operator to amend the machine's proposals.

FMS cell transport control

As flexible manufacturing system (FMS) cells are not entered by humans when in operation, transport inside the cell can be automatic. Transport can be provided by conveyor or by self-propelled transport units, the latter being essential for large and heavy items. Self-propelled units normally follow predefined routes within the cell between the various machines and the cell stores. A problem arises, however, when one of the mobile units breaks down, as it will be positioned on one of the standard routes. Either transport within the cell must be stopped until that unit is removed or the routes must be varied to allow the remaining units to go round the immobilised one. As the routes may cross and all routes overlap with others at each end, the routes which need to be altered depend on where that unit is on each route. If the unit breaks down close to a machine, there may be no alternative but to reroute the other mobile units and to revise the cell schedule to avoid the use of the blocked machine.

This is a transport problem which does not create safety difficulties and it is practical to add an IKBS 'alternative route finding' subsystem to the transport system software. It requires the cell geography, the start and end points of each route, the position of the immobilised unit (which is added into the cell geography) and rules for finding practical routes. These rules will contain knowledge on turning circles, width of the mobile units, clearances required and preferably route usage and time patterns to allow routes to be picked to minimise transport delays where one mobile must wait for another to get out of its way.

Removing 'flash' from moulded plastic

When liquid plastic is injected into a mould, some of the liquid penetrates the mould separation interfaces and sets as hard thin sheets. When the mould is opened and the items removed, each may have extraneous material or 'flash' attached which has to be removed. Often the flash cannot be removed by a process applied to the whole article since the articles may be fragile, with little difference in thickness between the flash and thin parts of the article. Furthermore, any such process would reduce the surface definition.

Where there are only a small number of products, a numerically controlled machine can be programmed to remove the flash, but this may not be worthwhile where there are short runs of 'specials'. The alternative is to provide a machine with a 'perfect' sample of the finished product which it can inspect and then use the knowledge it obtains from that inspection to make any other items which it receives identical to the 'perfect' one. If the machine makes its inspection unassisted, it will, in effect, search for flash across the whole surface of the article. There is no need for this as flash only forms at mould interfaces.

It is usually better, therefore, to fasten the sample in the machine and for an operator to trace out movements over its surface along the flash lines than it is to leave this task to an AI system. However, as the machine is loaded with articles from which the flash is to be removed, either they must be placed in an identical position to the first or the machine must 'know' what differences there are between the positions and allow for them. Identical loading is often difficult to achieve; a facility to determine positioning may be better.

The following steps are needed:
- set up:
  - surface scan of the 'perfect' sample by the machine
  - surface scan of the flash lines (under human guidance)
  - derivation of the information required to determine differences in position.
- Operation:
  - surface scan sufficient to determine differences in position
  - derivation of the flash positions relative to the machine's frame of reference
  - flash removal.

The surface scan could possibly be visual but touch is easier to provide. A separate scan machine will be required to avoid the need to change tools on the main machine. The first scan of the set-up stage is a complete non-intelligent search; the second scan is directed by the operator. The third item is an IKB system to work out what information establishes the position of an item. This will include redundant tests as the machine does not know which information will be found, nor in what sequence. Note that the flash positions are also used in this; if the articles were spheres, the flash would be the only distinguishing mark to establish their positioning. The first scan of the operation stage should terminate as soon as the machine can establish the position of an item and should be planed to obtain that information as rapidly as possible. This requires AI control. The remaining tasks are mechanical.

Selection of part-used sheet material

Operations such as profile cutting do not allow the use of sheet material to be pre-planned and result in the need to hold numbers of part-used sheets of different thicknesses, sizes and shapes. When a job is to be done it is difficult to select the best of the part-used sheets (to minimise waste) unless they are all manually inspected. An alternative is to note the size and shape of each sheet as it is returned and make the choice of sheet by machine. Shapes of flat sheets are easy to detect, particularly where they are moved back to store and so pass a common point where a shape detector can be sited. This could be a TV camera or any of a number of other possibilities.

The order for the required shape is usually by material, thickness and number required, with simple shapes such as circles or squares defined by dimension and more complex shapes by physical pattern. All these can be entered into a system simply. Material, thickness,

Manufacturing

number and simple shapes can be entered via a keyboard and patterns via a 'shape detector' like the one mentioned above (possibly the same one). An AI system can be used here as a two-step process.

The first step selects suitable sheets. For example, if one small profile is required and there are part-used sheets, one needs to select the smallest one which will fit the required profile. A full-sized new sheet would be an absurd choice.

The second step 'fits' the shape or shapes to the sheets and reports both the degree to which that sheet can satisfy the order and the size of the resultant waste. This information is then used to select a sheet combination which gives a satisfactory (but perhaps not optimal) solution.

Note that if this is done but the operators are not informed how the system fitted the shapes on the sheets, they will not be able to cut the required number from them. A print or display showing the sheet and the machine's layout of the shapes is needed to avoid further waste.

Some observations

There are so many, very different manufacturing processes that it is just not possible to give a fair representation of possible uses of AI in the manufacturing field in this short chapter. It is hoped, however, that the examples given have shown that AI is possible within the manufacturing field, and the reader should use them not as a definitive list but as guides in finding AI opportunities within his particular area of manufacturing.

As with other searches, it is useful to look at those places where the automatic process (or the machine) stops and a human is used and to answer the question 'Why is he there?'

In general, most opportunities for AI to be included in plant require it to be integrated by the manufacturer, so look particularly at areas which are 'special' to the installation rather than at standard bought-in plant which is used exactly as its manufacturer expected; and, of course, keep informed of progress made by the plant vendors.

Two of the examples given earlier illustrate the improvement of standard plant by the addition of AI modules. The FMS transports are normally controlled by standard numerical sequences which direct them along their normal paths. The AI module can generate new numerical sequences to keep the cell operational after a transport breakdown. The AI module is not physically connected to the transport. It uses information held by the transport control computer as input and feeds its results back to update the control data. Similarly, the voice-operated control module is an addition to a standard item. There are many machines which have multiple controls, allowing them to follow different sequences of operations under the operator's guidance. In some instances, as in the one described, performance can be improved by automating the sequences, provided the operator retains control. A small computer sited by the machine operating the controls can be an economic addition requiring little modification of existing plant.

The introduction of machine intelligence into a factory need not be a large-scale undertaking.

Summary

There is general recognition that intelligent machines can be used in manufacturing and an expectation that they will eventually become the norm. Though most of the publicity has gone to large, expensive purpose-built

Manufacturing

robots, there are other, less dramatic, cheaper ways of using AI. The five examples discussed were:
- a process control module
- a tool control device
- an FMS cell transport route planner
- a device for cleaning flash from plastic
- a system to select from part-used sheet.

16 Quality Control

The purposes of quality control include that of detecting material and products which are below standard. The examples in this chapter are taken from this area of quality control, where the task is one of inspecting and testing either all or samples of raw materials, finished products, partly completed items and components. Although the primary purpose is to determine whether or not the whole item is satisfactory, a secondary purpose with complex items is to locate the part or parts of a faulty item where the fault lies.

The testing of an item is usually a mechanical process. If it is computer controlled then the program will be conventional. This does not mean that there is no use for intelligence in this field; there are three different areas of quality control where intelligence is desirable. The first area where AI can be useful is in helping to decide how large a sample to test, what tests to apply and how to choose the sample from the population. The second area is in fault location and the third is in identifying the failure in the production system which caused the fault in the material or product. These three areas are each discussed below.

Selecting the tests

There is certainly merit in having a permanent minimum testing level and the tests and sample size are usually invariants specified for the product or raw material by the quality engineer. However, there are certain conditions which indicate that quality failures are more likely to occur at a specific time or that a particular component is unusually likely to be below standard. For example, if an unusually large number of errors of the same nature have recently been detected, one could infer a possible common cause, which may also have affected other items as yet untested, and conclude that these may also have the same fault. This would suggest more intensive use of the appropriate test to detect this fault.

Similarly, if a piece of plant has just been overhauled, one might conclude from that overhaul that there had previously been some risk of an error which could cause faults in the products coming from that plant. These errors would then be specifically tested for. There are many other similar causes of increased failure risk such as a change of material or component supplier, extensive overtime working, the pre-Christmas party season, lowered staff morale, a new employee in a key position on the production line or changes to the production sequence. One could write down a set of rules for the quality inspector and the testing laboratory directing them to apply additional tests under each of these conditions, but there could be many such rules. No one would remember them or remember to check whether the various conditions applied or remember to perform the calculations associated with valid rule combinations. An intelligent knowledge-based system connected to and informed by the corporate data base could do this job without additional input. It could learn of supplier changes, overtime working, absenteeism levels, new recruits and so on, and use this data in conjunction with its own rule base to suggest increased testing. It could request increased sampling of products from one particular production line or from batches incorporating suspect raw materials. It could identify the suitable additional tests to apply to either all or specific samples. When a computer system is used to administer the tests and to compare the results against a standard, it can report the current failure rates to the IKB system and in return receive its directions from the system as to which tests to apply.

Locating faults

Once a fault has been detected in an item, either the whole item is rejected or the faulty component(s) must be identified and replaced. This can be straightforward, but in complex products such as electronic equipment it can be difficult to determine which particular component has caused the faulty result.

Fault location is usually based on a knowledge of what the product structure is intended to be, the intended functionality of each component and a set of tests verifying the required functionality. It may also include knowledge of the failure rates of each component and their structural connections and knowledge of conditions which may have caused failure such as those discussed under the previous heading.

There are two common methods of fault location. One method is to proceed systematically through the item's hierarchy, testing each level in turn. For each structure in which a fault is found, further tests are made on each of its substructures until the 'reject and replace' level is reached. This method can involve the use of a large number of tests, and although it appears that it should locate any fault to the required degree of precision, it may not actually do so. For example, the fault could be caused by an input which is not allowed for in the tests, such as the item being violently shaken.

The second method is to use an informed guess as to the most likely trouble spot and test this. If a fault is

Quality Control

found, the component is replaced and the whole item is retested. If this does not cure the problem, then the next most likely trouble spot is tested.

Humans usually combine the two methods; at each step they know how probable it is that a knowledgeable guess will locate the fault, and then they attempt to choose the minimum-effort option. The combined method is often less effective than it should be as people tend to be optimistic as to their prospects of guessing correctly, particularly when they also built the product. Computer programming, for example, is a production process involving extensive testing. Programmers reguarly waste effort by believing that they can guess the location of a fault long after they have passed the point where they should concentrate on a systematic search.

The combined method, without the optimism, can of coure be built into a rule-based system. It is effective when used for repeat products where the structure is constant and the tests can be predefined. When the product is complex the time saved through more rapid fault finding can justify the system cost.

Fault cause identification

The quality of any product depends in part on the quality of the method which was used to produce it, on the materials used and the attitudes and skills of the individuals who were involved in the production process. Thus a fault can be created by any combination of the following:

- the plant used to produce it
- the materials incorporated in it
- the attitude, knowledge and skills of the operatives
- the standards and methods as applied by the operatives.

When a single fault is located during or at the end of the production process it is seldom possible to identify the root cause. For example, if the single fault lies in a bought-in component, it could be due to a fault in the component when received or it could be due to damage during the construction process. However, if a common fault is discovered in several different components irrespective of batch or supplier and the frequency is higher than that shown in previous sample tests, then the root cause is more likely to lie in the process than in the raw materials. The nature and frequency of faults considered in combination can give a valuable indication of the probable cause. This directs attention to parts of the production process needing attention. A system which is expert in diagnosing the causes of faults in finished or part-finished products can save considerable waste or rework and can also improve the general quality of the goods. The field of diagnostics in a classic expert system opportunity.

Combinations of the above

The three example areas discussed above are obviously related in the information which they use and to some extent the output of each can be used as input to the next. This is particularly true for the second and third application areas. An example of an expert system in which these two areas are clearly related is described in some detail by Mitra (2) in his paper on the identification of faults in plate glass. His system assists in the identification of particular faults and then goes on to suggest the root causes, such as damage to the furnace lining, impurities in the raw materials, and so on. The paper does include technical material, but it can easily be bypassed and the business problem and its cure can be appreciated without any AI training.

Summary

AI techniques can be used to improve the effectiveness of quality control in:

- the selection of tests and samples in view of prevailing conditions
- locating faulty components in complex items
- diagnosing the root causes of faults.

All three are related; the last two are closely related and can be built as a single unit.

17 Investment Decisions

This chapter is concerned with the selection of business investments, excluding portfolio assessment and optimisation. Portfolio assessment is a fruitful but specialised AI field which differs considerably from other business investment problems and so is not discussed here.

There are many ways of reaching investment decisions – too many to cover in this chapter. According to Carsberg and Hope (3), the three methods most favoured by large companies in the UK in 1973 were:

- qualitative judgement
- internal rate of return (DCF yield)
- payback period without discounting.

In 1977 Walton (4) found that 'payback' was used as the main method by over half the UK firms studied. Klammer (5) found that in the USA between 1959 and 1970 'discounting' moved into first place as the main method, 19 per cent using it in 1959 and 57 per cent in 1970; 'rate of return' and 'payback' were in second and third places. Clearly there is continual reassessment of method. In this chapter the three methods listed above are examined from an AI viewpoint with some quite interesting results.

Investment decisions are often interrelated. Individual opportunities may be mutually incompatible or supportive. Supportive investments may increase the individual benefits, reduce the overall risk or both. Interrelations are not discussed in this chapter.

Investment Decisions

When examining a single possible investment the objectives remain the same whichever method is adopted. These are:

- to estimate the cost schedule of the investment, regarding it as a 'probable' risk-related schedule
- to estimate the benefits if the investment is made (again, a combination of scheduled values and risks)
- to combine the estimates listed above into an overall valuation of the investment which can be compared with alternatives and used to reach a decision.

The choice of method of assessment determines the way in which the final objective in this list is achieved. This is demonstrated in the three following sections in which the individual methods are examined.

Qualitative judgement

Purely numerical methods require that all the information relevant to a decision is valued for arithmetic manipulation. Proponents of qualitative judgement consider that the work involved in producing those values is unjustified for the following reasons:

- The initial estimates are inaccurate.
- The end result of processing inaccurate data is an inaccurate answer.
- There is increased risk that someone will believe that the answer is accurate.
- Qualitative values such as 'very risky' have more meaning to the decision maker than some attempted numeric valuation of the risk.

This method allows the combined use of qualitative and numeric values. It is usual to use quantities when possible, even if it is expressed as a 'fuzzy' value such as 'about £10 000'. Summarising is used to reduce information volumes. The decision maker is supplied with notes or comments on the values which he uses to assess the accuracy of individual values and final totals.

The decision process is personal to the decision maker and no doubt varies, but in two instances examined in outline the process was apparently as follows. The decision maker used four groups of information which he held in his mind. These groups were:

- goals, objectives and policies to be achieved
- classes of investment, each with model values of associated benefits, risks, and costs (each class also had a standard model of an investment pattern or schedule)
- estimates of factors relevant to the business, such as market sizes, costs, risks, durations and prices which can be used to verify estimates in a proposal
- rules for evaluation; some procedural, others conditional.

The assessment is made in stages. The first step is to obtain an overall idea of the aims and nature of the proposal without going into detail. This may be done by looking at the index and then flicking through the document. The decision maker matches the aims of the proposal against his goals and uses his understanding of the proposal's nature to classify it and find a relevant class. Some class models carry clear 'reject' signals whilst others are marked as 'tentatively accept' as a result of earlier experiences. If the proposal activates a class model which carries such a signal, a preliminary decision is made at once. These initial decisions are seldom reversed, and the first step is clearly of primary importance in the assessment process.

The second step involves a scan through the detail. During this scan:

- Each item is checked against its 'pattern' and a 'credibility valuation' is made for that item.

Investment Decisions

- The items are built into an outline model of the investment proposal.
- The model is used to identify missing items, risks and so on by comparison with a standard model for that investment classification.
- A search is made for dominant items; that is, items which have a major impact on the decision by reason of magnitude or relationship to goals.

The third step finalises the decision:

- If an initial decision was made in the first step, then it may be overruled by a dominant item or if the 'model' is reasonably credible and very different from the class model.
- Where no initial decision was reached (i.e. the investment class has a neutral valuation), it may be made positive by a dominant item or if the proposal is both credible and profitable. Otherwise the investment is rejected.

The quality of the judgement, as measured by the probability that the decision maker will, on the whole, make decisions which are later proved to be cost-effective, appears to be determined primarily by the investment class information and secondarily by the business-oriented information which the manager holds rather than on the rules which he uses. This suggests that it would be worthwhile eliciting this knowledge from good decision makers even if it were used as guidance for human intelligence rather than built into a machine.

The construction of a model of the investment proposal, partly from the proposal itself and partly from the standard class model, appears at first sight to be very complex, and one would expect that an AI system which does this would be difficult to build. It is also doubtful whether such a system would actually be used.

The other place where AI techniques might assist in

this field is in processing the fuzzy numeric values for the decision maker. This would be a management tool rather than an expert system.

Internal rate of return

The internal rate of return is a purely numeric method of valuing projected investments which provides an interest percentage as its response. The cash flow associated with the investment is projected and then discounted to a present-day value (PDV) of zero by selecting an annual discount rate which produces that result. The annual discount rate which yields the zero present-day value is the internal rate of return. The method is simple and is often performed by iterating a discounted cash flow calculation with alternating high and low discount rates which give negative and positive present-day values, the discount rates being adjusted on each iteration to get closer to the desired zero PDV rate. The difficult part of the process is that of projecting sufficiently accurate cash flow forecasts.

Payback period without discounting

This is another method which uses the projected cash flow as input to a simple arithmetic process. The undiscounted projected cash flow values are added algebraically in time period sequence to that time period in which the cumulative value passes through zero. The elapsed time between the initiation of the investment and the time when cumulative cash flow passes through zero is the payback period. As with the internal-rate-of-return method, the difficulty is to produce the cash flow forecasts.

Estimating future cash flows

The problem with the two methods described briefly in the two preceding sections of this chapter is that of deriving a cash flow value for each time period from information which is inaccurate, often qualitative and incorporates a range of possibilities for almost every variable. When either of these two methods is used it is at the final stage in a process which includes a number of separate qualitative judgements. Those judgements are not concerned overtly with whether or not the investment should be made but rather with the assessment of a number of separate pieces of information to determine the value to allocate to some numeric item. For example, cash flow estimates include estimates of the value of the income in each future period. The information used for estimating may be qualitative information, such as the likely activities of competitors, the condition of the manufacturing plant and its influence on production capacity and possible changes in attitude by buyers in the particular market towards specific functions, price and delivery period.

The decisions which are made in the process of estimating cash flow values naturally determine the internal rate of return and the payback period. They are therefore an important part of the total investment decision. As these intermediate judgements are rarely made by the manager who is charged with determining whether or not to implement, and may not even be closely reviewed by him, the manager has effectively delegated part of the decision to those who prepare the proposal. This may not be in accordance with the manager's wishes.

If the individual intermediate qualitative judgements can be made using some or part of the manager's own expertise, the result will reflect more closely the decision which the manager would have reached had he done all the preparatory work in person. Since the approach breaks down the overall decision process into a number of separate tasks, and as each task is constrained to a limited field, each may be regarded as a prospective expert system in which the expertise is that of the decision maker, or at least has his approval.

The general contents of each such system is similar to but much simpler than that described in the 'Qualitative judgement' section early in this chapter. It is more practical since the solution to each sub-problem requires much less information and knowledge than the solution to the whole problem.

Acquisitions

Acquisitions and the purchase of significant holdings in existing companies are a special class of investment decisions with special difficulties of assessment. The investment projects discussed previously all start with a clean sheet, whereas acquisitions bring with them their previous history, which influences their future performance. They may have contractual liabilities; they have a financial position which may be obscure or contain concealed aspects; they have existing plant, stocks, products and development work in hand; they also have their own staff with their own capabilities, faults, attitudes and beliefs.

Successful acquisition is always uncertain, even for the most expert corporate investors. Much depends on the way the acquisition is handled following its purchase, so it is difficult to assess the accuracy of purchasing decisions until after the event. Yet despite the complexity of the task, it appears that successful acquisition experts base their decision on the same sort of process as was described in the 'Qualitative judgement' section. Moreover, it appears that there are a fairly small number of dominant rules which they apply during the first step, in which an initial, provisional decision is reached.

The authors have done no full studies on this problem, but from preliminary discussions it appears that an acquisition adviser based on the rules used by one or two experts could well be feasible.

Summary

Investment decisions always require a high level of expertise irrespective of the particular method adopted. Often critical intermediate decisions which have a profound influence on the final decision are made by subordinates who lack the manager's expertise. Expert systems may be a feasible and practical means of allowing the decision maker's expertise to be applied at critical points.

The construction of a complete 'investment decision-making expert system' is so large and complex a task that it would only be economic for large investors.

18 Fraud Detection

It is difficult to discuss fraud detection responsibly in a book. Any description of a method of defrauding a business might be used as a pattern by criminals. Similarly, any detailed description of a fraud detection system might result in a criminal changing his practices and avoiding detection. This chapter cannot therefore contain detail on either fraud or on counter-measures.

Fraud and other computer-related crimes represent a very high cost in many businesses, and AI technology can play an important role in controlling those costs. This operational area cannot, therefore, be ignored in a book such as this. The purpose of this chapter is to encourage businesses which are vulnerable to fraud to investigate the use of AI as a defence and to indicate a general approach.

Information and fraud

Information is one of the most valuable assets of a business. This is such an obvious statement that its truth is seldom properly appreciated. Anyone can see instantly that a business would die on the spot if it 'forgot' what was owed to it by whom or how it functioned. Yet despite that it is very easy to overlook the cost attached to the verification and transformation of information, the benefits of improving its accessibility and the risks of unauthorised access. The majority of business informa-

Fraud Detection

tion is now held on computer storage devices, although there may also be a security copy elsewhere, and in this form it impacts with fraud in two ways.

First, it is itself a prime target for fraudulent access. Change the computer-stored information and you have effectively changed reality, or at least changed it for long enough to take the money and run. And not just money. Almost anything from cars to spirits, machine parts to shiploads of oil, earth-moving equipment to weapons, can be stolen more comfortably and with less risk by changing computer-stored information than in any other way. There are even books on open sale which explain how to get past the standard computer defences, how to learn passwords, how to obtain access to computer software and how to change stored information. There is one such book in our office now, bought at a local newsagents. The defences of many on-line systems need strengthening against unauthorised access.

Second, information is a powerful defensive weapon which can be used to protect itself and other property. It can be used to detect fraud, to prevent damage and to identify the individuals who are attacking the system, even when they consider themselves safe miles away with their home computers and a telephone. To exploit the full defensive power of information one does need intelligence. Purely mechanical conventional systems are too predictable and too easy to circumvent. An intelligent system is neither.

Detection of fraud by an employee

Consider the following situation. The employee is a senior programmer in the data-processing department of a manufacturing company. He has access to the computer and can write his own programs. He is authorised to access the stored data and is informed as to the defensive procedures used by his employers; he may even have designed some of them himself.

He is also a thief and wishes to steal a small proportion of the product of the business on a regular basis. This is one of the hardest frauds to detect because the thief is forewarned of every defensive action. Moreover, as the proportion of dishonest data-processing professionals is very low, his attack will be unexpected. When a risk is low there is little justification for special expense to protect against it.

Consider how the fraud will be planned. Our man will have to go through or round the normal defences at least once if he decides to adjust the software – more regularly if he chooses to alter the stored information such as the control files. He can arrange all this; for example, he can engineer a breakdown in the software, stay late to repair it and bury his special routines in an apparently harmless utility program which is used every day. The software will still be apparently unchanged, the controls will balance and it would take a very skilled auditor to determine that the computer was involved at all. Things will disappear of course, but they will apparently disappear by pilfering from the stores. Actually they are going out of the factory in the company's own lorries complete with all the proper paperwork. If anyone starts to investigate in detail, the thief will know. He can even arrange for the system to tell him and so have time to dismantle his operation.

Now suppose that the business obtains an expert fraud-detection system; perhaps the managers arrange with another business that each will design and build one, and then exchange them. These systems might contain knowledge of the installation files and controls and have provision to update their own control files. They might have control over the data formats they use in their own files, switching between several so that those private data files are inconstant and thus incompre-

Fraud Detection

hensible to anyone who inspects them, however skilled. They might be able to select what they want to inspect, whether program or data, choosing at random and, of course, having the intelligence to check for logical consistency. If the information were stored on tape, retained by a security officer and used under his control at random or once each day, the thief would have no idea what would be inspected or when, and no way of finding out. He might well decide to find another, less careful employer.

Programmers will note that the system as described above could be circumvented. The description given is not quite complete and there are several ways of adding to it. As long as the installation staff do not know which additions have been made, it is effective. A system of this type would be able to detect other forms of fraud, not just internal fraud, and so should not be too expensive to build, in view of its possible value.

Fraud from a remote terminal

This is a simplified version of an 'aggressive defence'. Suppose that a business uses remote terminals connected through the public switched network of telephone lines to enter details of payments due. It is therefore at particular risk. The communications protocol software in the computer has been slightly adapted so that it can 'understand' either of two sets of rules for communication. One is completely standard, the other is standard with very minor differences in the messages sent by terminals. An analogy of the two sets of protocol rules, using English, might be that the terminal could use the standard procedure and start the conversation by saying 'Hello' and conclude by saying 'Goodbye' or use the special protocol for which the computer has been specially programmed and transmit

'Goodbye' at the start and 'Hello' at the end. The terminals owned by the business have been adapted to use the alternative – that is, 'Goodbye' – first.

If an unauthorised user attempts to communicate with the computer, he will naturally use the standard protocol. The computer can understand this, but identifies him instantly as unauthorised. However, it does not just cut him off; it lets him into a special part of the system, since if it did not he might keep trying until he found the correct way in. The special part of the system apparently responds to his attempts to break through the password protection. Actually, after a short struggle, it allocates him his own identifier which is used to help distinguish him and to relate him to any colleagues of his who may use it later. Once he is 'in', the expert system learns as much as it can about him from the options he chooses whilst the phone call is traced back and, sometimes, his local police are alerted. The system can suggest whether to call the police or leave him to implicate himself completely.

If he takes action to change data, the expert system monitors what the result of those changes would be were they applied to the real files and, if he appears to be attempting a fraud, he is allowed to proceed to obtain evidence of his intentions. The changes are applied to copies of records, not to the records themselves, to ensure that no damage is done unless the security officer decides to allow the change through to help trap the criminal.

Non computer fraud

Suppose that a hire purchase company is being troubled by a fraud in which the criminals:

– start a double-glazing company

Fraud Detection

- sell some windows and establish a legitimate agency
- include 'sales' to false clients among genuine sales
- obtain payment for sales to false clients
- maintain monthly payments for a period of a few months to avoid early discovery
- disappear, leaving a rented shop behind.

It is not possible to check up every agency every two months, which is all the time it takes to fraudulently collect some £30 000. The hire purchase company needs to be able to identify some smaller group of agencies which will include most of the criminal operations and then keep close contact with these. There are conventional means of identifying such smaller groups, but some criminals have found out how to avoid detection by them. A better defence is required.

Discussion with the company's investigators reveals that there are certain common patterns to these frauds. An expert investigator can, in time, pick out the doubtful cases even when they are not detectable by conventional systems. None of the pointers, when taken alone, are very selective, but grouped together they can be valuable. As there are real frauds along similar lines it is better to give no details here. Many of the pointers, however, can be obtained from the record of transactions between dealer and finance company, so an expert 'watch dog' can be incorporated into the processing software to give warning of any agency which it detects as a possible risk.

Summary

AI systems can be developed to assist in detecting fraud. They can also assist in identifying the person responsible for the fraud and in his entrapment. An indication of means, but no details, have been given. Organisations interested in applications in this field are recommended to work out their own approach, with help if necessary. A detailed published account of this area would be self-defeating.

19 The Staff Function

This chapter is included to illustrate the uses of AI technology in corporate services.

Corporate services use a small proportion of business resources. Possible savings and improvements are smaller than those in main-stream activities, but they are worth considering here for the following reasons:

- Corporate services can have a leverage effect on corporate efficiency.
- Large corporations have heavy services expenditure, even though small in proportion to the total.
- Service tasks include a significant proportion of suitably sized intelligent work.

Two staff-function tasks have been selected to illustrate the way in which one may search for suitable opportunities. The discussion is extended to exemplify the consideration given to leverage and variation which is necessary when assessing services opportunities.

Manpower planning

Manpower planning is not an area which brings immediate improvements in corporate profitability, but it is an activity which has significant long-term benefits. Ensuring that staff have the training and experiences needed to be effective takes years, with only partial benefit in the interim. Yet in the long term the motivation, skill, experience and 'business style' of key staff are the chief determinants of profitability. Thus improvements in this area are worthwhile, and any opportunities found should be included in the 'long list' even though they are unlikely to be selected for initial implementation.

Manpower planning should only be a problem in larger organisations. In the smallest, father knows he will hand the business over to son and plans accordingly. Some businesses use full manpower planning, including the identification of high-flyers at an early stage, the identification of alternative replacements for key positions and the estimation of replacement numbers required for less vital categories. For example, the UK health service plans the recruitment and training of general practitioners on a national basis having regard to retirements, emigration and immigration but plans the development of specialists and consultants in more detail on a regional basis.

Manpower planning is a part of business planning in which the most important components are:

- estimation of recruitment needs and turnover
- identification of key posts and preparation of replacement schedules
- comparison of requirement forecast with actual requirement in each category (shortfall identification)
- derivation of category recruitment and training programmes
- identification of candidates
- preparation of candidate training plans.

There are special problems in estimating recruitment needs and turnover in this field, and the risks attached to estimates are often large. In category planning the large population evens out individual variations but has no effect on changing trends due to staff behaviour and changes in the environment. The duration is often long.

The Staff Function

For example, a high level of apprentice recruitment may be set by a high turnover of both craftsmen and apprentices during their first five years. If a new factory opens in the immediate neighbourhood or an existing large employer closes down, the turnover rates may change significantly. The estimation of turnover and demand involves the use of uncertain qualitative factors: one of the indicators for an AI application. If there are known rules for handling those factors to deduce reasonable estimates then the task may be feasible.

With key-post planning there are problems on a parallel to those encountered in estimating recruitment needs and turnover. For example, the initial plan may provide for the replacement of a senior manager who is due to retire in five years. The plan may provide for two possible candidates each to receive appropriate experience over those five years on the expectation that staff turnover at that seniority is very low and it is most unlikely that either will leave in that time. If a year later one of those candidates has left, a further candidate would be identified for development, there being ample time in which to train him. However, if the turnover of middle managers has increased to 20 per cent per annum, it would be necessary to train four or five to have an even chance of one still being employed when the post becomes vacant. The cost of that training would be excessive.

The other tasks listed previously seem less likely candidates for AI solutions. They are either purely mechanical (e.g. the production of a key-post replacement schedule) or they are too complex for easy implementation (e.g. the design of a training and experience schedule). There may be opportunities for feasible assistant expert systems in the complex tasks, but these will only be profitable if there is a large training department.

Estimation of staff loss

('Staff loss' is used to mean the number of staff who leave the company.) The estimation of staff loss by category is normally based on the assumption that the current staff loss rates will continue unchanged. In practice the staff turnover of an organisation is seldom stable. If actual rates are plotted over a period of years one usually find that they differ significantly from time to time. These variations in rates have been studied extensively and are known to be determined by both external and internal causes.

External causes include the general trade cycle, local changes such as the actions of competitors drawing on the same labour pool, variations in transport facilities or real estate prices. Most of these changes can be predicted in advance with sufficient accuracy and the rules relating them to staff loss are well developed.

Internal causes are usually dominant and are equally well known. Many relate staff loss with morale. For example, one theory relates morale to corporate size and structure, suggesting that a company can grow only to a certain size with any particular structure and management method. As that maximum size is approached, loss rates increase, thus causing it to contract again. If this theory is accepted, then there is a tendency for loss rate and size to be related. A company which is expanding may need to take account of this relationship in its planning. There are many other internal factors under management control which influence loss rates. Some, such as the level of internal communications, are very tenuous; others, such as the rewards in the form of increased salary, holiday entitlement and so on, are easier to measure and have better-defined relationships with turnover; many are interrelated.

The application appears to be feasible. The possible benefits depend on the size of the training program and the extent to which staff loss and recruitment variations cause undertraining or overtraining. If the benefits would be valuable, then the next step (writing down the main rules in English) could be taken.

Staff allocation

The task of identifying the correct person to fill a particular role varies widely in significance and complexity. For many jobs any suitably qualified individual will do, but for a few key posts the success of a whole business area is decided by the extent to which one individual meets the demands made on him. Key posts are often managerial and require management skill, drive, mobility and other typical management attributes. Others require unusual combinations of attributes, and it can be difficult to find the individual in a large organisation who is best suited to the work.

The problem lies in the need to choose from qualities which are not easily quantified. Personnel records can be machine searched for quantified attributes but not for the information contained in textual reviews. A large organisation could require each section and department to provide information on staff who have special qualities. There would be resistance since such people are needed wherever they are, but although some would be concealed, it would be possible to create a register containing most of them.

The rules required to classify individuals according to their suitability to particular posts would not be constant. A basic set of general rules might be stated, but variations and additions would be required for most searches. This is not a serious disadvantage for intelligent systems, as new rules can be added very easily.

The principal difficulties with this application are in the establishment of the register and in selecting those special skills which are to be recorded. The AI system which searches the register is not difficult to build. The benefits depend on whether company policy gives preference to the selection of the best person for key positions or to departmental staff autonomy.

Summary

Two illustrations from the staff function have been discussed in this chapter. AI techniques can be used profitably in the service functions of large companies, but benefits and feasibility of application areas vary widely. Although the applications appropriate to a company will differ and in many instances a successful application in one company will not be feasible in another, most large organisations should have several AI opportunities open to them.

20 Retail Banking

The principal objectives of the high street bank are:
- to increase its customer base
- to increase the deposit value which can be used to generate profit
- to increase the use of services by customers
- to avoid client delinquency.

Its key resource is the knowledge which its staff have of the neighbourhood, of its clients and of their financial situations and needs. This is supplemented by banking and financial knowledge and skill. It is constrained by many factors (including public perception of what is proper for a bank), by corporate restrictions imposed to protect the bank and by legal restrictions to protect the public. Each branch is required to conform to bank standards and has little discretionary freedom except in clearly defined areas. No single branch can adopt a new method such as the use of AI technology; this must be a general decision.

Retail banking is supported by service functions concerned with buildings, staff recruitment and development, stationery, computer services and many others, each of which are large organisations in their own right. In each of these areas there are opportunities for the profitable use of AI technology. However, the two objectives selected for discussion in this chapter are both taken from the principal branch activities, namely:

- increasing sales of services
- reducing client delinquency.

These two are closely related. Client delinquency can be reduced by correct selection of the services and their values supplied to clients. Both depend on accurate knowledge of the customer, in the one case to know what he needs and when he needs it so that it may be sold to him, whilst in the other the information is used to decide what he can afford. The first task is therefore to examine the information available on individual customers.

Customer information available

Customer information is obtained when the account is opened, and there are opportunities to obtain updates and further details when additional services are requested. Most banks limit the information held in computer-readable form. The 'home' branch keeps additional information on paper in the individual customer's file, but its value is limited because:

- information on customers is difficult to acquire
- there is no way of keeping it up-to-date
- document held information is difficult to access.

In addition to the above, there is the financial information held on the account which includes details of recent transactions, account balance, overdraft provisions, cross-reference to other accounts, and so on.

Desired-customer information

For every service which a bank offers one could define the characteristics of the ideal prospect. For example, the ideal prospect for house insurance is someone who is on the point of buying a new home and who has not been sold insurance by his solicitor or estate agent. If we had a list of people about to buy new homes which showed the date of intended purchase and the property values, we could concentrate on those, tailor the proposal correctly, offer to call round and discuss their needs and so sell more house insurance at a lower sales cost. Similarly, more loans could be sold if we knew who needed a loan, how much he would need and when he could pay it back. Research has shown that life assurance sales literature which offers a single correct sum secures a much higher acceptance rate than generalised literature which shows a table of different sums. Selling is always more productive when it is correctly focused and the offer is tailored to the prospect's real requirements.

To ensure that customers are not offered more than they can repay, one needs to know their future income and expenditure, their assets and their liabilities.

With both these groups of information available, the profitability of retail banking could be improved dramatically. This is enough potential to justify heavy expenditure if there is a reasonable probability of success.

Data protection and privacy

Clearly if the extra information needed is to be obtained, it must be held in computer files. Since our subject is AI, those files will contain information that is not entirely factual; some of it will be inferred. Moreover, the obvious place to obtain the basic information is from transactions passing through the account. Legislation, ethnics and business prudence restrict the use that can be made of personal information. Information which can be related to a single individual may only be used for purposes authorised by law or agreed by him. However, information which cannot be traced back to an individual can be used for any purpose desired.

Thus information stored through a one-way algorithm may be analysed freely since it cannot be related to the individual from whose account it came. This process can be used to learn the characteristics of different classes of customer even if there is only one in the class. However, once the characteristics of a class are known, they may only be used to classify customers who have consented to being classified.

AI technology can be used to identify prospective buyers of the various services offered by a bank. It can indicate the value of the services that they will probably wish to obtain, and it can be used to indicate the safe limit of credit which they should be allowed. But its use should be restricted to customers who have agreed that the bank may monitor their accounts and use transaction and other information to assist in giving financial advice. Such agreement would normally be forthcoming as most people expect to obtain financial advice from their bank, but it is important to respect their right to decide.

Obtaining the information

The information needed depends on the services offered. Two illustrations are used below, one being house insurance and the other loans to arable farmers. In both cases the inference is made using two sets of information. One is the general characteristics of the classes which are relevant and the other an extract of the transaction details of each customer. The class characteristics are determined by:

- identifying known members of the class
- passing copies of their transactions through a one-way algorithm
- determining the class characteristics.

Retail Banking

The class characteristics are then used to search the account transaction and static information of consenting customers to find matches.

Prospective buyers of house insurance

Two indicative classes relevant to house-insurance buyers are discussed below. There are others, but these two illustrate the method adequately.

One class of house buyers moves regularly every two or three years, often changing locality and generally buying a more expensive house each time. They become more stable when their salaries reflect their promotion progress and house moves occur on a delay after a salary uplift from their previous move. They make regular mortgage payments by standing order or direct debit. They are more likely to be employed in business or industry than by a practice; generally speaking, lawyers, doctors and dentists rely on personal recommendation and move less often.

If the accounts of members of this group are analysed, there is stronger correlation between salary size, rate of increase, payments of a mortgage, and so on, between group members than there is among the general population. However, the regular interval between changes of address is definitive.

The sample can now be used to derive the rules which identify members of this class who are likely to be thinking of another move. Some of the rules are:

- Those who have moved regularly related to time are likely to continue the pattern.
- Those who have moved regularly related to salary are likely to continue the pattern.
- Those who are nearing the age of forty are less likely to move.

- Those who have children (related accounts) of between eleven and eighteen are less likely to move.
- Those with small mortgage repayment to salary returns are more likely to move.
- The value of the next house will be approximately the value of the present one, plus salary increase since last move times a multiplier, less mortgage repayment times a multiplier.

A second classification can be obtained by studying the payments of a local sample who have recently moved. Many house buyers pay for house surveys and examination of a localised group of movers will show correlation between moving and payments to a group of accounts. That group will include structural, wood, electrical and drains surveyors. Surveys are paid for about the same time that the new purchase is due and so are good indicators of serious intent. There is also correlation between survey fees and property value.

Having obtained a list of 'possible move identifiers', by examining the remaining population and looking for these 'identifiers', one can select those customers who may be in the process of moving and thus be in a position to offer them house insurance for the right amount at the right time.

Loans to arable farmers

The branch staff should know who amongst their customers are farmers. If there is doubt they can be readily identified by taking a sample of known arable farmers and searching for correlated payments and receipts. Payments will be made to seedsmen, agricultural engineers and similar specialists whilst receipts will be paid by corn-chandlers and others.

Arable farmers require loans for specific purposes at seasonal times, where 'season' refers to both date and farming conditions. Thus loans may be required for fertiliser and seed and they will be paid back after harvest. The amount of the loan is determined by current prices; the cultivated area remains constant. Thus when some farmers make arrangements for loans, the ratio of these loan values compared with the value of previous loans is likely to be a constant ratio for all farmers. Those farmers who have not requested loans can be identified and a suitable loan offered at the right time and for the right amount. This may prevent a proportion of farmers from looking elsewhere for their funding.

Summary

Two representative objectives of branch banking were examined for AI technology opportunities. In both cases an improvement could be made by inferring more about individual clients. Subject to the need to respect confidentiality, the required inferences can be made through an account survey using rules derived from correlation exercises.

References

(1) T.L. Maney and I. Reid, 'An Efficient Embedded Inexact Matching Implementation', unpublished, available from Data Logic Ltd.

(2) S.K. Mitra, 'The Identification of Defects in Glass', proceedings of the Fourth European Conference on AI, Pisa, Italy, 1984.

(3) B. Carsberg and A. Hope, *Business Investment Decisions Under Inflation,* Institute of Chartered Accountants, 1976, Chapter 8, pp. 43–49.

(4) M. Walton, 'The Investment Decision: Theory and Practice', *Economics,* Autumn, 1978.

(5) T. Klammer, 'Empirical Evidence of the Adoption of Sophisticated Capital Budgetary Techniques', *Harvard Business Review,* vol. 50, pp. 387–94.

(6) J.R. Quinlan, 'Discovering Rules by Induction from Large Collections of Examples', in D. Mitchie (ed.), *Expert Systems in the Micro-electronic Age,* Edinburgh University Press, 1979.

(7) J.R. Quinlan, 'Inferno: A Cautious Approach to Uncertain Inference', RAND Note N-1898-RC, RAND Corporation, Santa Monica, CA 1982.

(8) G. Polya, *How to Solve It,* Doubleday Anchor Books, New York, 1957.

Further Reading

Non-technical

To get a general, non-technical understanding of the artificial intelligence field and at the same time enjoy several hours of intellectual pleasure, try D.R. Hofstadter, *Gödel, Escher, Bach: An Eternal Golden Braid* (Penguin, London, 1979). The book is worth reading for its own sake, whether or not you are interested in AI. It is certainly non-technical in that it assumes no previous knowledge, yet it takes you through art, mathematics, music, genetics and much else with poetry as a guide. It is indescribable; just enjoy it!

To get some understanding of the relationship between human and machine intelligence as so far developed, and a fairly painless introduction to some of the most famous developments in AI, read Margaret Bowden, *Artificial Intelligence and Natural Man* (Open University Press, Milton Keynes, 1977). Margaret Bowden is a psychologist and, of course, her book looks at the subject of AI from that viewpoint.

Betty Edwardes' book *Drawing on the Right Side of the Brain* (Fontana, London, 1982) is about non-reasoning intelligence. It describes how one can make a major improvement in one's ability to draw, and explains her theory of how the step change is achieved. She supports the view that the right side of the brain does not work by inference but in other ways. The subject matter is interesting and it is a good source of ideas on non-reasoning intelligence.

Technical

The UK Alvey programme has published an excellent document on the field of IKBS and on their objectives and plans for developing AI titled 'Intelligent Knowledge-based Systems – a programme for action in the UK'. Copies can be obtained from the Alvey Directorate, Millbank Tower, Pimlico, London.

The vast majority of books available on AI are concerned with its history and theory; the expert systems discussed are large systems such as Mycin and Dendral. There are a few books, however, which look at the subject from a more 'practical' viewpoint. Three of these books are listed below. There are more available and the following is intended as a cross section rather than a definitive list.

Mike James, *Artificial Intelligence in BASIC* (Newnes, Sevenoaks, 1984). This explains the central ideas of AI and uses programs written in BASIC to illustrate the methods discussed.

John Krutch, *Experiments in Artificial Intelligence for Small Computers* (Howard W. Sams, and Co., Inc., 1984). This is similar to the above but slightly more theoretical. The illustrating programs are written in Microsoft 11.

Chris Naylor, *Build Your Own Expert System* (Sigma Press, Wilmslow, Cheshire, 1983) and Halsted Press, (John Wiley, New York). This is less of a 'history of AI' than the above two, although it does describe the more famous expert systems such as Mycin. It helps you to decide systematically what you want and how to go about building it.

Index

Accountancy 17
Accountants 105-6
Acquisitions 160-1
Artificial Intelligence (AI) 4, 8, 11-15
Atomic software 21

Banking 16-30
   See also Financial institutions, Retail banking
Batch sizing 126-7
Business analysis 59
Business factors 119
Business planning 119-24

Cash flow 108
   see also Profitability
Cash flow (estimating) 159-60
COBOL 28
Competition (business) 119
Computer fraud 163-6
Consultants (AI) 31, 32, 35-40, 43, 44
Control (of a system) 76, 77
Conventional systems 65-7, 77, 112-13, 148
Corporate services 169-74
Cost effective 65, 70, 78, 157
Credit control 102-10
Credit limits (establishing) 103-7

Credit (minimising) 108-9
Customer information 176-81

Data base 13, 112-15, 117
Data protection 177-8
Debt
   See Credit control, Credit limits (establishing), Credit (minimising)
Departmental management 32, 35, 36-43
Design 68-73, 77
Development 65-77
DCF yield 154
   See Initial rate of return
DP 36-43

Employee (AI) 32, 33
Errors (in system development) 74, 75, 77
Evolution 68-71, 76, 79
Exception report 113, 115-17
Expert system 4, 8, 13, 21, 45, 55, 60-1, 161, 164
   See also IKBS
      Assistant 5, 8, 14, 15, 70, 72, 114, 119
      Consultant 5, 8, 13, 15, 69
      Creative systems 45, 52-5
      Idiot savant 5, 8, 135
      Interface 5, 8, 114-15

Explain (expert systems which can) 89

Factoring company 24
Failure analysis 132-3
Fault location 148, 150-2
Feasibility 41, 43, 44-55, 57-8, 60, 62, 75, 161
Financial institutions 106-7
　See also Banking, Retail banking
Flash 142-4
FMS 138, 141-2
Forecasting 119-21
Foreign exchange 17
　See also Nostro reconciliation
Frame (knowledge block) 7
Fraud detection 162-8
Fuzzy search 117, 157

Growth (system) 75-6

High volume I/O 12, 14, 20, 54, 69, 111

IKBS 7, 150
　See also Expert system
In house expert (AI) 32, 33
Income (increase) 89, 90
Inference engine 7
Information 5, 13, 54, 111, 162-3, 175
Initial rate of return 158
Insurance (house) 179-80
Intelligence (machine) 12-14, 36, 39, 148
Investment decisions 154-61

Knowledge 5, 12, 20, 45-8, 52-4, 120-1, 122, 164
Knowledge base
　See Rule base

Language understanding 50-1
　See also Natural language understanding
Learning systems 53, 105
LISP 8, 12
Loans 180-1

Maintenance planning 133-4
Management information 66, 111-18
Manpower planning 169-71
Manufacturing 137-47
Market shortage (foreseeing) 96-7
Market size 119
Market surplus (foreseeing) 96-7
Market survey 120
Mathematical models 91, 120, 155

Natural language interface 114-15
Natural language understanding 106
　see also Language understanding
Non computer fraud 166-7
Nostro reconciliation 16-30
　See also Foreign exchange

Object oriented language 8
Opportunities (in business) 31-43

Index

Pascal 29
Patterns (identifying) 119, 156
Payback 154, 158
Plastics 142-4
Preventive maintenance 129-36
Privacy
 See Data protection
Production 137-47
Production scheduling 124-8
Production systems 148
Profitability 1, 8, 11, 30, 56-8, 63, 78, 87, 90-1, 109, 138
PROLOG 8, 12, 24, 26, 28
Prototyping 24, 29, 45, 66, 68-73, 75, 77, 79

Qualitative judgement 154, 155-8, 160
Quality control 148-53
Quality engineer 149

Reasoning 47-8
Reports 112, 118
Requirements specification 65
Research 76
Resource (forecasting) 119
Resource requirements 119-22
Retail banking 175-81
 See also Financial institutions, Banking
Robotics 6, 8, 45, 51-2, 55
Rule base 7, 61, 121
Rules 105, 109, 120-1, 140, 156, 160

Sales 87-94, 109, 119, 120
Sales aid (portable) 93
Salesmen 87-8
Salesmen (travelling) 88, 89

Sales order entry 87-94, 109
Sales order frequency (increasing) 93
Sales order priority 92
Sales order revenue 87
Sales orders (by post) 88
Sales orders (by telephone) 88, 89
Scheduling systems 125-7
Senior management 32, 35, 36-43
Service (improving) 87, 91
Service (monitoring) 92, 127
Sheet material 144-5
Shell 7, 14, 79-80, 120
Short list 56-64
Small businesses 78-81
Software construction 73, 77
Software engineering 21, 54-5
Software houses 80
Speech input 114-15
Speech recognition 6, 8, 45, 49, 55, 138, 141
Staff allocation 173-4
Staff function 169-74
Staff loss (estimation of) 172-3
Stand-alone systems 12, 15, 120
Stock consumption (monitoring) 96
Stock control 95-101
Stock delivery periods (monitoring) 97
Stock positioning 99
Stock replacement 95-8
Stock supplier (selecting) 97
System development department 32, 34

Testing (products) 148-50

Testing (systems) 73-4, 77
Tools (development) 67, 71, 77
Transport 137

Warehouse loading 99-101
Warehouse retrieval 99-101
Warehousing 91, 95-101
Wish list 41